MIDLAND RAILWAY ARCHITECTURE

Typesetting by:
Aquarius Typesetting Services, New Milton, Hants.

Printed in Great Britain by:
Biddles Ltd., Guildford, Surrey.

Published by:
Oxford Publishing Co.
Link House
West Street
POOLE, Dorset

MIDLAND RAILWAY ARCHITECTURE

A Pictorial Record of Midland Railway Stations

V.R.Anderson and G.K.Fox

Oxford Publishing Co

INTRODUCTION

The Midland Railway was incorporated by Act of Parliament on 10th May 1844 by the amalgamation of three railways, the Midland Counties, the Birmingham & Derby Junction and the North Midland. All three had received their respective Acts of Parliament in 1836. The two former companies had opened parts of their lines in 1839, the latter in May 1840.

At the time of its incorporation, the title 'Midland Railway' was quite appropriate although had it been known then how widespread its lines and influence would become, perhaps another name would have been considered.

Numerous lines were built, purchased by or amalgamated with the parent Midland Railway culminating with that of the London, Tilbury & Southend Railway in 1912. By this time, it was possible to travel under Midland auspices by using joint lines and running powers from Stranraer in Scotland to Bournemouth in the south and to Lowestoft and Shoeburyness in the east and Swansea in the west, to say nothing of the railways operated by the Company in Northern Ireland.

It is, perhaps, inevitable that the names of Francis Thompson and Sancton Wood should feature prominently in the early period of Midland Railway Architecture. However, the days of the individualistic design seemed, for the most part, to be numbered after the 1844 amalgamation due to the Midland Railway's preference for employing architectural staff in their engineering department. Most Railway companies had a Chief Engineer or Engineer in chief, as the Midland preferred, an identity usually inferring that the occupant was a person qualified in civil engineering.

The man arguably the most responsible person for setting the seal on design for a distinctive house style which lasted throughout the life of the Company was John Sidney Crossley, who was appointed Engineer to the Midland Railway in 1858, to succeed Charles Liddell. These styles had a far reaching effect on railway architecture in general influencing designs for well over half a century.

The pattern for building solid structures with sympathetic use of local materials started with the construction of two lines which were obviously planned before the formation of the Midland Railway, but namely the Nottingham to Lincoln line of 1846 and the Syston to Peterborough route of 1846-1848.

That which followed is well documented elsewhere, and readers are recommended to the many authoritative works on the subject of the Midland Railway should they wish to delve more deeply into the detailed history of the Company.

We have chosen to circumnavigate the lines of the Midland Railway in England and Wales, showing a haphazard selection of stations. Our working is from Bath, Bristol and Swansea to Birmingham, on to Derby then for a trip to the western seaboard of the Midland Railway's empire at Morecambe, and a visit to the Settle to Carlisle line, before returning south via Leeds and Rotherham to Nottingham. Finally, we take a run up the main line to St. Pancras.

The Midland Railway looked after its passengers, and was arguably the most considerate and progressive of the companies at the great majority of its stations.

Midland Railway Architecture is inevitably concerned with views from or of passenger stations. Limited coverage of other installations is included, as well as examples of the many and varied structures encountered in the vicinity of stations.

The aim of the authors has been to extend the coverage given to the subject by its companion volume *A Pictorial Record of LMS Architecture*.

V. R. Anderson, Poulton-le-Fylde
G. K. Fox, Bredbury, Stockport

ACKNOWLEDGEMENTS

We gratefully acknowledge the kind help and assistance of the numerous people who have made this publication possible.

Our sincere thanks go to Mr R. J. Coon, C. Eng., F.I.C.E., S.C.I.T., Regional Civil Engineer BR (LMR) and Mr P. J. White, C. Eng., F.I.C.E., Area Civil Engineer, Manchester BR (LMR), to those who have placed their photographic collections at our disposal and those who have generously given their valuable assistance, in particular Mr Arthur Austin. Finally, again, to our respective wives, Valerie and Jacqueline.

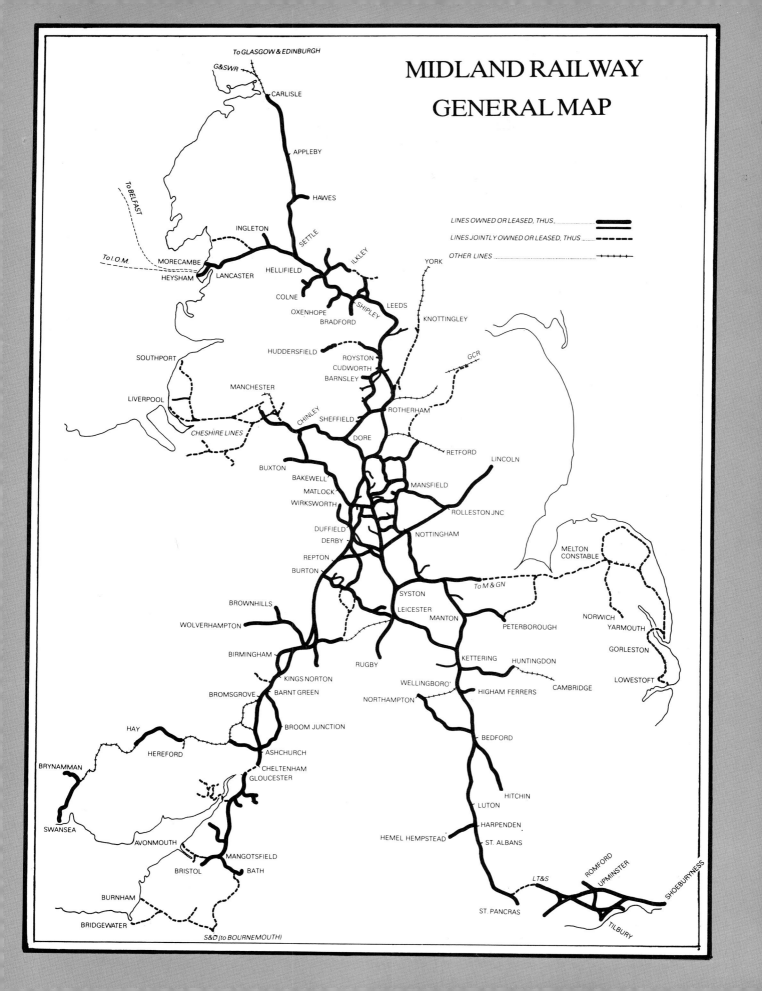

Bath

Plates 1 & 2: Slender Ionic columns under a ballustraded parapet balanced by the decorated iron port cochere mark the imposing classical frontage, in complete sympathy with the Georgian traditions of the City of Bath (*above*). This frontage block was attributed to the architect J. H. Sanders, working under the direction of the Company engineer, J. S. Crossley. This building contrasts with the simplicity of the arched iron train shed constructed by Andrew Handyside and Co. of Derby (*below*). The station is, arguably, one of the finest of the smaller stations in the country. The whole has been sympathetically renovated and preserved by a supermarket organisation.

Bath to Bristol

Although a branch to Bath had been considered many years before, it was not until 1864 that a Bill was placed before Parliament for a line from Mangotsfield to Bath. The chosen route along the valley floor crossed the River Avon many times. The line was opened from Mangotsfield to a temporary station at Bath in August 1869 for passengers, and in September 1869 for freight. The permanent station, built in classical style, was opened on 7th May 1870. On the western side of the town, it was conveniently placed for the fashionable residential area.

The authorised extension of the Somerset & Dorset Railway from Evercreech to Bath opened in July 1874. From that time the Somerset & Dorset and the Midland Railway shared the Bath station. The title 'Bath (Green Park)' was not bestowed until June 1951, and prior to this it was unofficially known as Bath (Queen's Square).

The route from Bath Station immediately crosses the River Avon on a lattice girder bridge (*Plate 4*), a design originally used for all the river bridges. Although most were later changed to a plate girder type allowing for heavier engines, the bridges at the station remained, but were strengthened in the early 1930s.

The extensive locomotive depot jointly used by the Somerset & Dorset Railway was immediately west of the river crossing, on the north side of the line opposite the freight facilities. The single S&D line branches off in a southerly direction at Bath Junction, 41 chains from the terminus

About a mile from Bath was Weston. The building was of the twin pavilion type, seen in many guises throughout the Midland Railway system during Crossley's reign as engineer.

Plate 3: Bath

Plate 4: Bath

Plate 5: Bath. This view of the departure platform shows the glazed end screen of the train shed, and the matching side arcades to good effect, whilst illustrating the limited platform cover provided. Of the four lines entering the train shed, the two outer ones served the platforms, with facility for some carriage storage on the centre pair.

Plate 4: The motive power depot can be seen beyond the lattice bridge.

R. J. Essery

Plate 5: Weston. The twin-pavilioned main building shows extensive use of elaborate fretted barge boards and the pierced iron canopy support in the recess between the pavilions. In contrast, is the wooden-framed waiting shelter. The palm trees add tropical overtones to a typical English railway scene.

L&GRP, Courtesy David & Charles

Plate 6: Weston. This view towards Bath shows the very long platform to the main building, and the footpath to the opposite platform. Of interest are the 'standard' Midland level crossing gates. The 3/8 in. diameter vertical iron bars were a unique feature.

Lens of Sutton

Plates 5 & 6: Weston

Plate 7: Kelston possessed a building style different to the others on the line, with rugged simplicity.

L&GRP, Courtesy David & Charles

Plate 8: Bitton. The main building on the southbound platform is reminiscent of the structure at Weston, although the shelter on the other side is of the cruciform stone-built style, with gables echoing the main building.

Mowat Collection

Kelston Station, at 4½ miles, was not opened until 1st December 1869, and only simple stone-built facilities were provided. Bitton Station was a building similar to that provided at Weston. However, at the former (*Plate 8*), there were more extensive goods facilities. The goods shed was characteristic of many Midland sheds in the south-west corner of the system, in fact the shed and station were copied at Thornbury, a branch built about the same time. North of Bitton, the excavation of a deep cutting yielded much of the building stone for the bridge and station construction along the branch.

The remaining intermediate station at Warmley had uncharacteristic structures, possessing short platforms and timber buildings.

For much of the way to Mangotsfield the Midland branch closely followed the course of the former Avon & Gloucestershire Tramway, constructed to carry coal from Coalpit Heath to the River Avon at Keynsham, to connect with the Kennet & Avon Canal Navigation, which itself became absorbed by the GWR.

The Bath Line Act contained clauses to protect this tramway, whilst also empowering the Midland Railway to negotiate with the GWR for the transfer of

continued on next page

Plate 9: Warmley

Plate 9: Warmley. This station appeared to suffer from a lack of planning, showing variations of building styles with haphazard location. This early view shows the 1899 footbridge with timber stairways. This provided a public right of way for pedestrians if the level crossing gates were closed. By 1912, it was found necessary to close-board the lattice work.

Lens of Sutton

Plate 10: Warmley. A similar but much later view, showing the replacement plate girder footbridge installed in 1929, and the LMS Hawkseye style nameboard. The round-headed windows and shallow-hipped roofing with extended eaves were features perpetuated at numerous locations, often in masonry. The dark coloured building on the right was a later addition, and is typical of the small timber goods sheds provided by the Company about the turn of the century.

Lens of Sutton

Plate 10: Warmley

continued from previous page
all or part of the tramway. However, negotiations fell through.

Mangotsfield Station occupied two sides of a triangular junction and opened with the Bath branch in 1869, superseding a station half a mile to the north. Platforms occupied the south side for branch trains and the west for main line trains. The lines to the east allowed through running to or from Bath and the north.

From Mangotsfield, trains from Bath entered the main line and ran over the route of the original Bristol & Gloucestershire Railway, opened in 1835 as another line to carry coal from Coalpit Heath, but this time to Bristol Docks. Later proposals for extension to Gloucester saw the name changed to the Bristol & Gloucester Railway, but more of this later. The most northerly of the intermediate stations on this part of the line, Staple Hill, opened on 1st November 1880. Some three miles before Bristol was Fishponds Station, which opened as Stapleton on 1st April 1866 but was renamed in July 1867. In addition to the two main platforms, there was a bay on the 'down' side.

Passenger services from Bath were carried into Bristol St. Phillips Station, opened in May 1870 to relieve the GWR & Midland joint station at Temple Meads. The single platform here was covered by an extensive ridge and furrow awning. St. Phillips, and all the stations to Bath closed when passenger services ceased on the Bath branch on 7th March 1966. Kelston Station had, however, closed in 1949.

Plate 11

Plate 12

Plates 11 & 12: Mangotsfield. A good early example of glass and iron roofing, but not of the more familiar ridge and furrow type. The lightweight lattice girders were supported on slender cast-iron columns. The feature of this longitudinal construction was the hipped ends and small finials.

Lens of Sutton and C. G. Maggs

Plate 13: No. 45589 *Gwalior*, with the 'Devonian' at Mangotsfield in April 1962, passes the Bath branch junction. The commencement of the branch is indicated by the 'O' milepost to the right of the picture. Mangotsfield Station signal box controlled workings to and from the branch.

G. Coltas

Plate 13

Plate 14: Staple Hill. In a shallow cutting near the southern end of Staple Hill Tunnel the Midland Railway provided this small station in 1880, with a collection of unremarkable buildings. The enamelled notice suspended from the bridge entreats the traveller to use the bridge.

C. G. Maggs

Plate 15: Staple Hill. A view looking north, along the approach ramp to the 'up' platform. The lattice girder footbridge spans the cutting, with support in the form of two brick piers. The diagonal fencing was a typical Midland (and later LMS) feature.

Lens of Sutton

Plate 16: Fishponds. The distinctive features of the brick building on the left are partially hidden by the canopy. The design of this building was repeated at Moseley, King's Norton and Water Orton. The canopy is of the later type, utilising transverse rolled section beams supported by cast columns and small undecorated brackets. Compared with the earlier view in *Plate 17*, this canopy has obviously been extended.

C. G. Maggs

Plate 17: An early view of Fishponds. The brick-built cruciform waiting shelter received improvements in the form of a heavy timber canopy supported on cast-iron brackets. The Fishponds nameboard is of an early Midland enamelled type; white letters on an Oxford blue background, held in a chocolate brown painted frame.

Lens of Sutton

Plate 18: St. Phillips. No. 41240, on a Bath local train, awaits departure in 1951. An odd assortment of structures was utilised to extend the accommodation of the station.

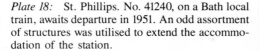

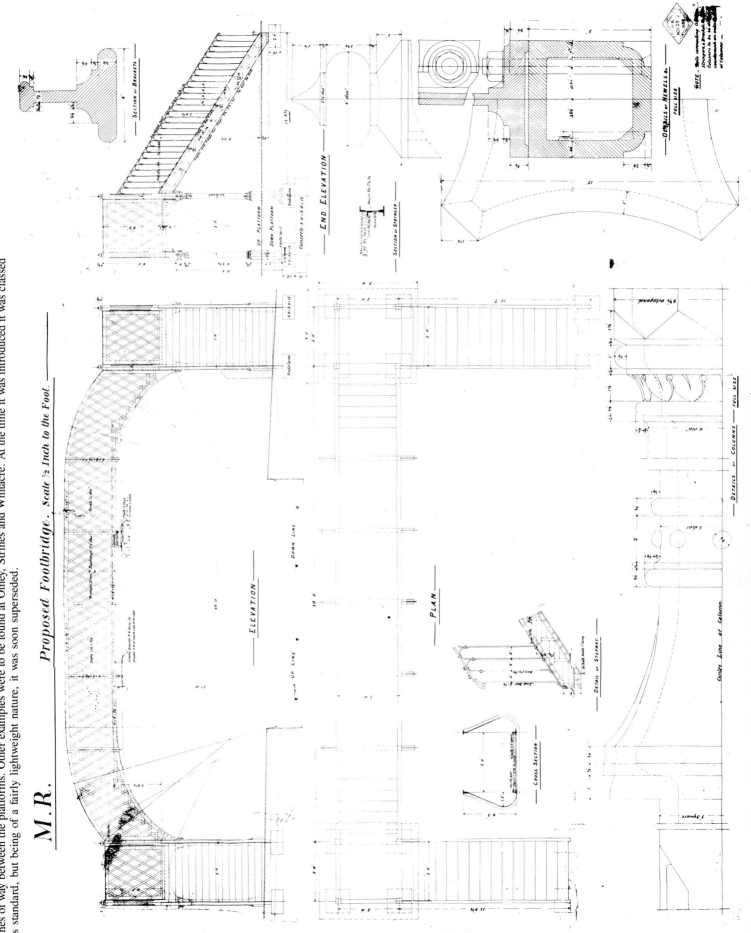

Figure 1: Yate footbridge, from an official drawing. A wrought and cast-iron elliptical-arched footbridge, introduced in the 1870s, to span two lines of way between the platforms. Other examples were to be found at Olney, Strines and Whitacre. At the time it was introduced it was classed as standard, but being of a fairly lightweight nature, it was soon superseded.

M.R.

Proposed Footbridge. scale ½ Inch to the Foot.

Plate 19: Yate

Mangotsfield to Gloucester

With GWR help, the Bristol & Gloucestershire Company obtained powers for an extension to Standish Junction in July 1839. At this time, the Company title was shortened to Bristol & Gloucester Railway. Isambard Kingdom Brunel of the GWR was appointed Engineer. This, and the financial help from the GWR made that company consider the B&G to be one of its dependants. Construction commenced in 1841, but by 1843 consideration was given to laying the track to broad gauge standards and a connection was allowed to the GWR station of Bristol (Temple Meads). However, as the tunnel at Wickwar and many overbridges were well advanced, these were never to full broad gauge specifications. Opened throughout on 6th July 1844, the line was worked by Stothart, Slaughter & Co. of Bristol. Late in 1844,

continued
on next
page

Plate 19: Yate, one of the original stations, had features in common with others on the Bristol & Gloucester Railway. Highlighting this is the Brunelian appearance of the station building with its flat continuous awning on four sides, steep-gabled roofs, and tudor doors, windows and chimneys. Matching subsidiary buildings on the 'up' platform were provided. The branch to Thornbury opened, after delays, on 2nd September 1872, and left the 'up' side immediately north of Yate Station.

Plate 20 (below left): Yate, looking south, in 1948, and pictured from the road bridge. The footbridge featured in *Figure 1* is prominent.

Plate 21: Yate. The cramped appearance of the goods yard belies the fact that this layout is repeated at other locations. The turntable allowed extensive use of the limited facilities. The medieval features of the goods shed are again repeated at Berkeley Road, Frocester, Charfield and Wickwar. The road overbridge has obviously been extended, as the original section is silhouetted behind.

L&GRP, Courtesy David & Charles

Plate 20: Yate

Plate 21:

continued from previous page

negotiations took place to amalgamate the Bristol & Gloucester Railway with the narrow (standard) gauge Birmingham & Gloucester Railway agreement being concluded by January 1845. Offers were made by the GWR to absorb the combined company but the Midland Railway were able to better the GWR cash offer, resulting in the Midland being granted a perpetual lease of the line from Birmingham to Bristol from 1st July 1845. Broad gauge remained south of Gloucester, the Midland Railway purchasing the Stothart, Slaughter & Co. engines.

At this time, trains entered Gloucester over part of the broad gauge Cheltenham & Great Western Union Railway from Standish Junction. By 1845, the Midland Railway were authorised to convert the Bristol & Gloucester section to standard gauge. This was completed, a new line laid parallel with the C&GWU (now part of the GWR) north from Standish Junction to a new standard gauge through station at Gloucester, and through running commenced in May 1854. Mixed gauge rails remained south of Standish Junction for many years.

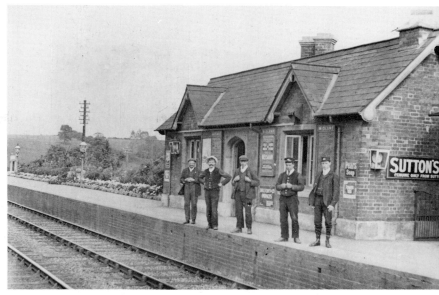

Plate 22: Wickwar. The station buildings do not appear to be original, but have conflicting features reminiscent of the Midland gabled pavilioned style shown in the gable roof extensions, and also with the Tudorescent Brunelian door frames and chimneys. The structure in front of which the staff proudly pose was repeated immediately to the right but was set back a few feet.

G. Dow Collection

Plate 23: Wickwar looking south. The large goods shed can be seen in the background. Again, an enamelled nameboard is in evidence. Note the simple timber waiting shelter on the 'up' platform.

Plate 24: Charfield. Apart from the absence of a footbridge, this view could almost be taken for that at Yate. The large detached stationmaster's house is worthy of comment and, although another Brunel item, it was not to his usual practice.

L&GRP,
Courtesy David & Charles

Plate 25: Berkeley Road. The sweeping curves take the Bristol line to the left and the Sharpness branch to the right of this June 1914 view, photographed from the signal box in connection with permanent way alterations. The corrugated-iron lamp hut was another standard Midland Railway item.

Ashchurch

Plate 36: This 1904 view shows the newly-completed overbridge carrying Tewkesbury Road over the railway at the southern end of Ashchurch Station. Work commenced in 1902 to replace the previous single span bridge of 1840. Construction was of brick and steel, with four steel stanchions and sill completing the central pier. Steel girders with brick jack arches made up the deck carrying the roadway. The bridge number, 25, is painted on to the brickwork and this illustrates a variant of the bridge numbering systems used by the Company, later standardised by utilising rectangular iron plates with cast numbers. Official engineering records identified this as the Gloucester and Birmingham line, and bridges, culverts etc., were numbered from the Gloucester end. Note the inside key chairs to the track of the siding. To the left of the central pier can be seen the platform serving the Tewkesbury branch, which opened in 1840 utilising a single carriage drawn by horse power. Under an Act of 1860, the Tewkesbury & Malvern Railway extended the branch to join the GWR at Malvern; this became Midland in 1876. Ashchurch Junction signal box, which features prominently in *Plate 37*, is hidden by the bridge pier.

Plate 37: The branch to the right is the line to Broom Junction and Barnt Green. This branch opened in sections; the Redditch Railway from Barnt Green, incorporated in 1858 and opened in 1859 was vested in the Midland Railway in 1874; Ashchurch to Evesham opened in October 1864 and the Evesham & Redditch Railway opened between 1866 and 1868 and became Midland in 1882. Midland standard fittings are much in evidence, such as the swan-necked water crane, corrugated-iron lamp hut, buffer stops, and the signal box name of cast letters on a wooden board attached to the front of the box. The platform canopies were a later addition. The footbridge is of a similar construction to that at Berkeley Road, and was erected in the same year, 1883. The signal box on the 'up' side, in the distance, is Ashchurch Level Crossing and controlled a rail link between the Redditch and Tewkesbury lines.

Plate 36
Plate 37

In contrast to the uniformity of the stations on the Bristol to Gloucester line, the ones illustrated here, north of Gloucester, have little in common, save for such detail as dressed lintels and door arches. Original facilities were minimal, resulting in the need for extension by the Midland Railway, and all show additions spanning many years of development.

Plate 38: Bredon received a new office extension, decorated with herring-bone brickwork, lozenge windows and carried a valance akin to that on the timber building at Berkeley Road and at Wadborough (*Plate 41).* The nameboard is of the Midland angled variety, with screwed-on cast letters.

Plate 39: Eckington had another variety of nameboard, this time a flat one, but again with cast letters. The simple waiting shelter, with extended valanced canopy fronting a flat roof, is of a style found at many locations.

Plate 40: Defford, this time with an enamelled iron nameboard. Although this is an early view, the canopy on the waiting shelter has had to be cut back to avoid fouling the structure gauge.

Gloucester to Birmingham

Heading north from Cheltenham, through Ashchurch, we are on the course of the Birmingham & Gloucester Railway incorporated by an Act of Parliament which received Royal Assent on 22nd April 1836. The line was to run from a junction with the London & Birmingham Railway at Aston, with rights to use the L&B station at Birmingham. Construction work started in 1837.

The route finally decided upon involved passing over a steep incline through the Lickey Hills at Bromsgrove. This was occasioned by the fact that local opposition prevented the railway running through Worcester, but also disliked the idea of a route further to the east, which could have avoided the incline.

A further Act of 15th May 1837 authorised a branch from Ashchurch to Tewkesbury, and provided for the Gloucester & Cheltenham Tramway to be jointly purchased by the Cheltenham & Great Western Union Railway and the Birmingham & Gloucester Railway.

The line opened in stages in 1840; Cheltenham to Bromsgrove in June, Cheltenham to Gloucester in November, and Bromsgrove to Cofton Farm, south of the Cofton Tunnel, on 17th September 1840. When the tunnel was completed, the line opened through to Camp Hill in December, Cofton Farm Station then being closed. Cofton Tunnel was finally demolished and the line was opened out from 26th-28th January 1929.

B&G trains commenced running into the L&B station at Curzon Street on 17th August 1841, but by 1842 it was considered expedient to build a station at Lawley Street for the use of B&G trains. The years 1845 and 1846 saw, respectively, the amalgamation with the Bristol & Gloucester Railway and absorption by the Midland, as mentioned previously. However, before we proceed to Birmingham let us divert westwards to the Midland Railway in South Wales.

Plate 41: Wadborough. The two timber buildings had similar characteristics to the one at Berkeley Road. The nearer one, however, does not have the roof extension and fretted valance. This 1956 view shows the Hawkseye style nameboard fitted by the LMS in the late 1930s.

H. C. Casserley

The Midland in South Wales
Swansea

Plate 42: Coal discharging equipment of the Midland Railway
at the coaling arm of King's Dock, Swansea, in 1922.

Plate 43

Plate 44

Plate 45

Plate 46

The Midland in South Wales

Anxious to tap the wealth of the industries of South Wales, the Midland Railway found it unprofitable to run trains over the metals of other companies. Running powers were available to Swansea over the GWR, via Hereford and Abergavenny. To ease the situation, the Midland Railway searched for an independent route to Swansea. Considerable traffic could be expected to and from districts served by the Midland Railway, such as ironstone from Northampton to Swansea, and anthracite from the South Wales pits to the Burton upon Trent breweries.

The semi-bankrupt Hereford, Hay & Brecon Railway had had a chequered career, and was worked, at the start, by the contractor who built the line and later by a succession of different companies. This line offered an excellent northern link approaching, as it did, close to the Midland Railway's Birmingham to Gloucester line at Stoke Works, near Worcester. In spite of ill feeling by the GWR concerning movement of passenger trains, use of their Hereford station was eventually established to give passengers direct connection with GWR trains.

The Hereford, Hay & Brecon Railway received its Act of Incorporation in August 1859. It was opened in sections between June 1863 and September 1864. The western end of the line was at a junction with the Mid-Wales Railway, just north of Three Cocks Station. Midland running powers over the HH&B commenced on 1st October 1869, with the lease of the line being granted in 1874, and complete absorption in 1886. Agreement was reached to run Midland trains over the Cambrian (Mid-Wales Railway) and the Brecon & Merthyr Railway from Three Cocks Junction into Brecon.

continued on next page

Plate 43: Swansea. The exterior of the Midland station, known for some time as St. Thomas.

Plate 44: Swansea, showing a view looking along the arrival platform.

Plate 45: Upper Bank, looking towards Glais. The motive power depot stands in the middle distance.

Plate 46: Clydach-on-Tawe. The station extension to the right is of similar construction to the building at Gwys, shown in *Plate 50*.

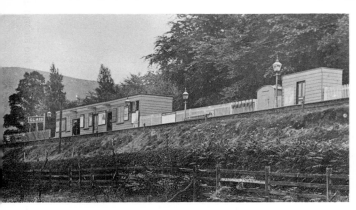

Plate 47: Glais possessed features more akin to Midland practice; note the angled nameboard above the diagonal fencing.

Plate 48: Pontardawe, looking north in 1905.

L&GRP, Courtesy David & Charles

continued from previous page

Attempts to lease the Brecon & Merthyr Railway failed in 1873, so the Midland Railway leased the Swansea Vale Railway by the Midland (Swansea Vale Lease) Act of 1st July 1874, and by an Act of 11th August 1876, the line was vested in the Midland Railway.

This small railway had opened during 1860/1, with an extension to Brynamman in 1864. The lease, as confirmed, allowed the Midland Railway to continue the running powers which the Swansea Vale Railway had exercised over the Neath & Brecon Railway from Ynysygeinon Junction, 12 miles north of Swansea, to join the Brecon & Merthyr Railway, west of Brecon Station. By an Agreement in 1877, the Midland Railway took over the running of the N&B's Ynysygeinon Junction to Brecon section, leaving the N&B the short section to Neath. The Midland Railway were forced to make many improvements to the Neath & Brecon Railway, and to double the main line of the Swansea Vale Railway.

At Swansea, powers were obtained to run over the Swansea Harbour Trust lines to carry coal to the coaling arm of the King's Dock.

continued on next page

Plate 49: Ystalyfera. A stone built station reminiscent of many to be found in the Welsh Valleys but more particularly on the LNWR. The characteristic feature is the canopy restricted to the central part of the building.

Plate 50: Gwys on the single track extension to Brynamman.

Mowat Collection

Plate 51: Cwmllyn Fell an unpretentious timber platform fronts a rudimentary brick shelter.

Mowat Collection

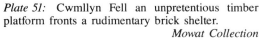

continued from previous page

Through workings of passenger and freight trains commenced in July 1877, and continued until the end of 1930. At this time, the heavy through freight workings had been transferred on to the Central Wales line of the LMS. Local passenger trains continued to run between Swansea and Ynysygeinon, and between Hereford and Brecon.

Architecturally speaking, there is nothing of note on the Midland sections of the line from Hereford to Swansea. Originally, most of the stations offered nothing more than waiting shelters. Even the St. Thomas terminus at Swansea was little more than a collection of timber buildings. The Hereford, Hay & Brecon Railway stations had much in common, all being timber buildings, although none offered many facilities except the station at Hay, which was the junction for the Golden Valley branch of the GWR. The section from Hereford to Three Cocks Junction remained part of the London Midland Region of British Railways until 1950.

Plate 52: A view of Glasbury-on-Wye Station, looking towards Hereford.
L&GRP, Courtesy David & Charles

Plate 53: Hay-on-Wye looking towards Brecon. The footbridge is of similar design to the one featured in *Figure 1.*

Plate 55: Whitney-on-Wye. The canopy was a unique feature.
G. Dow Collection

Plate 54: Hay-on-Wye. A local train arrives from Hereford. The engine crew are about to take on water in readiness for the climb towards Brecon.

Plate 56: Eardisley, another variant of the simple accommodation at the stations on this line. The large proportions of the angled nameboard should be noted. The junction is with the Great Western Railway.

Plate 57: A view of Kinnersley Station, looking towards Hereford.
L&GRP, Courtesy David & Charles

Plate 58: Moorhampton, showing a view towards Hay-on-Wye. The enamelled nameboards are an early example of what is thought to be a standard BR design, although their use was not widespread.

Plate 59: Credenhill Station looking east. The building was extended at the right-hand end by the LMS. Use is being made of the end loading dock in the goods yard (*cf Plate 112 at Edale*)

Plate 60 (above): A view looking towards Bromsgrove.

Plate 61 (below): The approach to Blackwell

Returning now to our route north towards Birmingham we reach the formidable barrier of the Lickey Hills. The Birmingham & Gloucester Railway breasted this obstacle by an incline of just over two miles at a constant gradient of 1 in 37.5. This figure is indicated on the gradient posts at the top and the bottom, although it has been documented at 1 in 37.7 and 1 in 37¾.

Plate 60: A view looking south from the top of Lickey incline towards Bromsgrove. This peaceful scene belies the effect created by hard-working motive power on an ascending train. Banking engines returned to Bromsgrove, making use of the crossover in the foreground. To the extreme left is the post indicating the change in gradient.

Plate 61: Immediately on reaching the top of the Lickey Incline trains enter Blackwell Station.

Plate 62: Blackwell Station. The brick building is a classical Midland structure of the twin pavilion type, the two wings linked by a covered area fronted by a glazed screen so reminiscent of many other Midland stations, particularly Whitwell. The hipped-roofed pavilions are not seen as frequently as the gabled type, although the hipped roof allows the prolific use of fancy eaves brackets. Again in evidence are numerous items familiar to the Midland Railway scene, including gas lamps, milepost, wall lamp brackets, loading gauge, and enamelled nameboard, as photographed in January 1907.

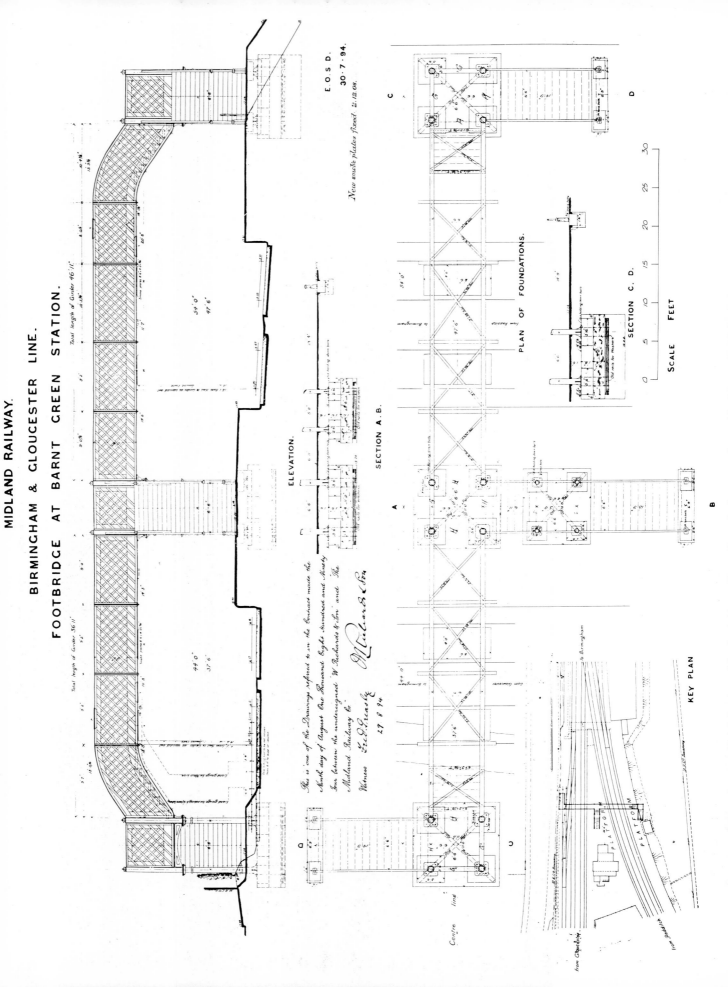

Figure 2: An official drawing of the footbridge at Barnt Green Station, manufactured by Messrs W. Richards & Son of Leicester. The design was a departure from the more traditional semi-elliptical profile, setting the precedent for future footbridge construction.

Plate 63: Barnt Green Station, as approached from the Gloucester direction. The 'up' platform is in the distance and connected to the 'down' and main station facilities by the footbridge. On the right can be seen the waiting shelter for the Redditch branch, which is featured in *Plate 66.*

Plate 64: Barnt Green. A Bristol express approaches from Birmingham. The waiting shelter beyond the signal box carries two cowled chimneys, a fairly common Midland feature. The cattle dock to the right has basic similarities to that detailed in *Figure 13*.

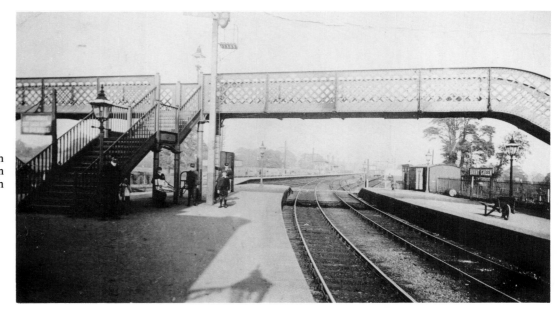

Plate 65: Barnt Green. A photograph showing the footbridge detailed in *Figure 2* as viewed from the branch platform.

Plate 66: Barnt Green. The station main building in the apex of the 'V' was completely different to any other structure on the line. It is richly decorated with dentilled brickwork and stone-dressed window surrounds. The waiting shelter to the right is in complete contrast, its only outstanding point being the heavy cowled chimney.

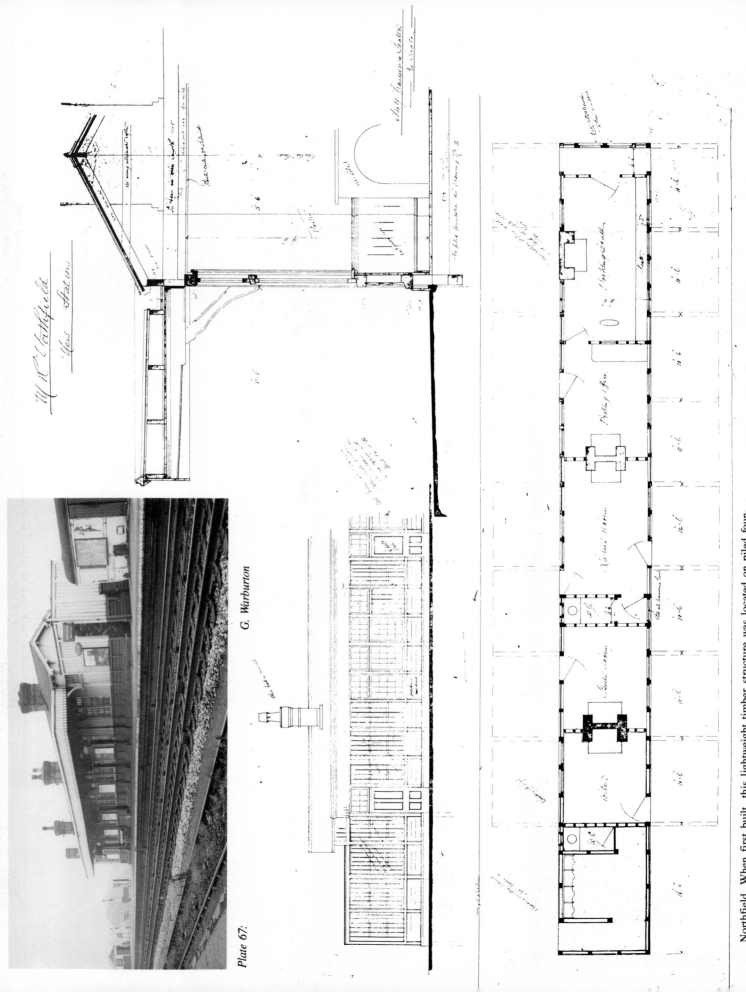

Plate 67:

G. Warburton

Northfield. When first built, this lightweight timber structure was located on piled foundations on the new embankment created for the widening of the line in 1893. *Figure 3 & Plate* at the Gloucester end of the platform. However, in 1898, a more convenient entrance was

Plate 68: An early view of Northfield after it had been found necessary to improve booking facilities.

Lens of Sutton

Figure 4: Details of the enlargement carried out during 1902/3, which involved enlarging the booking office and the provision of a new waiting-room at the Birmingham end of the building. Once the ground had become consolidated, brick platforms were provided, and it was possible to erect the new extension on concrete footings.

Plate 69: Details the waiting-room extension.

G. Warburton

Plate 68

Plate 69

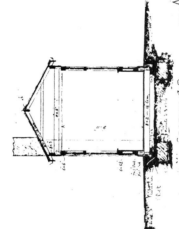

— M.R. NORTHFIELD. —

— SECTION A.B. —

— ELEVATION NEXT UP PLATFORM —

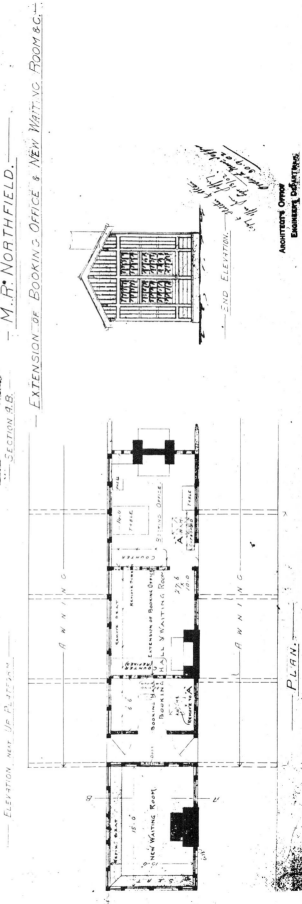

— EXTENSION OF BOOKING OFFICE & NEW WAITING ROOM &c. —

— END ELEVATION. —

— PLAN. —

ARCHITECT'S OFFICE
ENGINEER'S DEPARTMENT

Plate 70: King's Norton. The need for extra accommodation gave an unusual assortment of small buildings on the 'up' platform. This centre brick waiting shed is that shown in *Figure 5 (below)*. These small cruciform or cross-gabled shelters became an almost classic Midland feature, and were to be found at many locations.

We have already come across one at Bitton, and others appeared as far north as Ingleton and Bentham. Obviously, building material and construction detail varied to suit the situation. Only their minimal size caused them to be overshadowed by the larger and more illustrious main buildings.

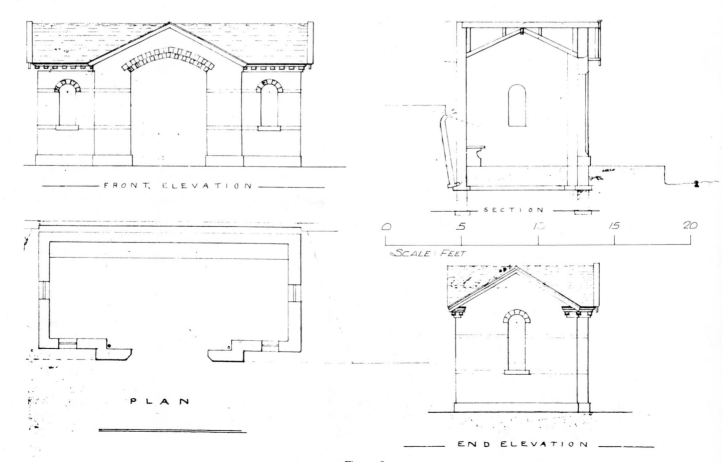

DRAWING for WAITING SHED KING'S NORTON

FRONT ELEVATION

SECTION

SCALE: FEET

PLAN

END ELEVATION

Figure 5

King's Norton was first opened by the Midland Railway in 1849 as a small wayside station with limited facilities. The waiting shelter depicted in the drawing (*Figure 5*) possibly originated at the time. Subsequent enlargement found the need for better accommodation, which was provided in a three-gabled building similar to that detailed in the drawing (*Figure 6*), and shown on the 'down' platform to the right of *Plate 70*.

A Birmingham West Suburban line had opened from Granville Street near the city centre to King's Norton in 1876. An Act of Parliament in 1881 allowed a tunnelled connection to the Birmingham (New Street) Station of the LNWR, and by 1885, Midland main line trains were running along the course of a modified west suburban route through New Street.

Further new works had provided widening to four tracks south of King's Norton, through Northfield, to Barnt Green from 1893, with goods lines outside the passenger lines. Extension north through King's Norton was not completed until 1926, when the station appeared as in *Plate 72*.

Plate 71: An early morning view of King's Norton in 1914, looking in the Gloucester direction. Unsophisticated milk distribution methods are evident as churns await passage into Birmingham. Again, we have an example of the kind of footbridge found at Ashchurch and Berkeley Road.

W. Rear Collection

Plate 72: A view photographed from the same spot as that in *Plate 71*. This 1950 view shows the results of the widening and rebuilding in the mid-1920s. The buildings carry all the typical Midland features, although of LMS construction. Note the changed footbridge; this plate girder type was installed to coincide with the new works. Midland Railway gas lamps are still in evidence on the 'down' platform.

L&GRP, Courtesy David & Charles

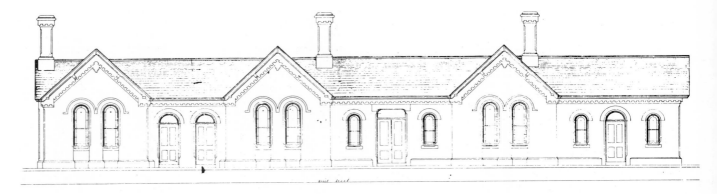

ELEVATION NEXT RAILWAY

DRAWING FOR STATION BUILDINGS AT BALSALL HEATH AND KINGS NORTON

SCALE FEET

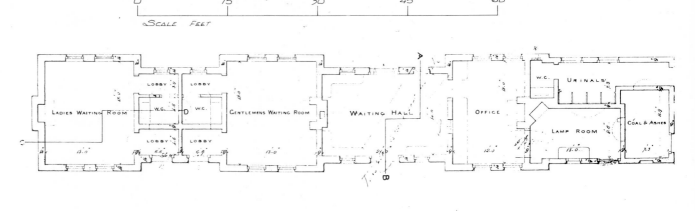

GROUND PLAN

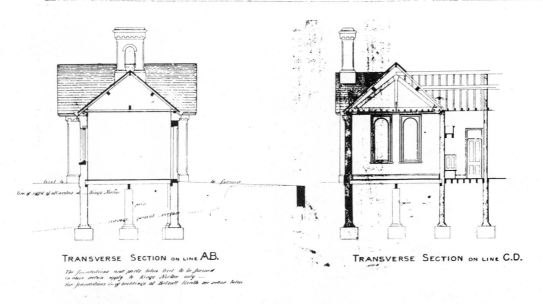

TRANSVERSE SECTION ON LINE A.B.

TRANSVERSE SECTION ON LINE C.D.

Figure 6: This drawing is based on information from an official drawing for a building to be placed at King's Norton and Balsall Heath. The latter did not materialise, and King's Norton appeared as a 'mirror image'. A true representation of this drawing was erected at Moseley (*see Plates 73 & 74*).

Plate 73: A view of Moseley, looking south towards King's Norton. This was the second station to carry this name and did not open until 1st November 1867, on the same day as the original Moseley, south of the tunnel, which had opened on 17th December 1840, was renamed King's Heath. King's Heath must have been rebuilt about this time, as the building was of the same overall design and layout, with detail differences to window and door headings and chimney stacks. In the foreground is a good example of standard 'unclimbable' fencing.

Plate 74: Moseley looking towards Camp Hill. Note the small cantilever roof waiting shelter; a very basic structure because of the limited clearance. The station could be approached by ramps from the high overbridge carrying Woodbridge Road.

Lens of Sutton

Plate 75: Brighton Road. In contrast to the deep cutting at Moseley, Brighton Road was located on an embankment, and this is reflected in the construction of the lightweight timber buildings and timber trestle platforms. The design of the buildings is typical for this period, and reminiscent of the timber structures already discussed. Ths station opened to passengers in November 1875. All the stations mentioned here closed on 27th Janaury 1941, although permanent closure of King's Heath was not finalised until November 1946, suggesting some wartime activity.

Camp Hill was, for some time, the terminus of the line from Gloucester. However, in 1846, connection was made with the Birmingham and Derby Junction line of the Midland Railway, allowing running into the centre of Birmingham, or through to Derby. Coaches for Birmingham could be detached here from Derby trains. Camp Hill continued to be a principal goods handling point. Prior to 1904, this station was known as Camp Hill & Balsall Heath. The station featured in this illustration was opened in 1867.

Plate 76: This scene is evocative of the Edwardian period and strong in Midland influence. The main building is again of the twin pavilion variety, but with the platform side roof continuous between the pavilions, and with a glazed screen affording passenger protection. This design is contemporary with the stations built at Nuneaton (Abbey Street) and on the joint line to Ashby, and of stations built for the southern part of the London extension. Of the many Midland items prominent is the rustic platform seat. This was painted in a chocolate shade, the name being painted white on an ultramarine panel. The castings for these seats were originally provided by Messrs Andrew Handyside, and the style later became standardised by the LMS when the parts were made at Wolverton.

Plate 77 (above): A view of Camp Hill, looking north; a scene some three years later after reconstruction of Highgate Road Bridge, the parapet of which is immediately to the fore of the main station building. The platform has been raised to accommodate the new main girders. The waiting shelter to the left is of the timber variety, with sloping roof and decorative sloping panel boards. In the distance can be seen wagons at Highgate Coal Wharf.

Plate 78 (below): Camp Hill, with the newly-constructed bridge to the right of the station. The station approach road is to the left. The projecting wing on the road side of the building is evident. The ground plan of this type of building was to be repeated when designs were sought for the Settle to Carlisle line, although these were provided with gabled pavilions.

Plate 79

Plate 80

Birmingham to Derby

Having bypassed Birmingham, we now find ourselves on the course of one of the original triumvirate of the Midland Railway. George Stephenson surveyed the area in 1835, prior to the Birmingham & Derby Junction Company's Bill being authorised by Parliament on 19th May 1836. Lines were to extend from Derby to Hampton on the London & Birmingham Railway's main line to London, and to Birmingham to the L&B terminus at Curzon Street.

Attention was concentrated upon the 'branch line' to Hampton, in order to secure as much of the London traffic as possible to steal a march on the Midland Counties Company, whose line to Rugby would be in direct competition. Robert Stephenson was the Engineer, and the line was opened to the public on 12th August 1839.

Trains were reversed at Hampton to reach Birmingham, or through coaches carried on to London by the L&BR. In less than a year the M&C opened and the Birmingham & Derby Junction Railway monopoly lost, as tolls to the L&B were heavy. The Birmingham & Derby Junction Railway now set about constructing the direct line to Birmingham, using an Act of 1840 to reroute from Whitacre through Castle Bromwich to a terminus at Lawley Street. The line was quickly built to open in February 1842. After this, the line to Hampton was reduced in status and soon became a single line branch.

Plate 81
Plate 82

Plate 79: Saltley. The island platform principle applied at Saltley consistent with new works around the turn of the century, which included in 1895 the removal of a level crossing and substitution by an overbridge 'Saltley Viaduct'. The facilities provided were housed in a timber building with large canopies, a design repeated some years later at Water Orton (see *A Pictorial Record of LMS Architecture* published by OPC).

Lens of Sutton

Plates 80 & 81: Castle Bromwich. Widening schemes and a direct line to Kingsbury, completed in 1909, resulted in a number of new works items, including a reconstructed station at Castle Bromwich. A view at rail level (*Plate 80*) shows the two timber-framed buildings with vertical board infill and large cantilevered canopies; a heavier construction than was usually found. The stairway and timber-covered footbridge led to the road level booking hall (*Plate 81*). This lavishly-decorated building in brick and terracotta was of a style fashionable with the Midland Railway at this period. Compare Bingley (*Plate 147*), Rotherham (*Plate 165*) and Cricklewood (*Figure 24*).

Plate 82: Water Orton, as it was before the 1909 widening scheme. Again we have the three gabled building seen at King's Norton and Moseley.

Original stations on the route from Birmingham to Derby were built at Castle Bromwich, Water Orton, Forge Mill (for Coleshill), Whitacre, Kingsbury, Tamworth, Barton & Walton, Burton and Willington.

Powers were sought in 1846 to form a junction with the LNWR to allow the B&DJR (now part of the Midland Railway) to run into the Curzon Street Station, and also for a line on to the Birmingham & Gloucester line. Lawley Street closed to passengers in 1851 when services were diverted to Curzon Street, and later on to the New Street Station.

Plate 83

Plate 83: Burton on Trent, looking north, along the 'down' platform. This island platform layout opened in 1883 when an overbridge replaced a level crossing. The original station on the Derby side of the level crossing stood from 1839 until 1883. The new station had a large entrance block on the bridge built in brick and timber, and with an open balcony overlooking the platforms. The platform canopy is of the traditional ridge and furrow type carried on lattice girders supported by cast columns. Although a much heavier structure, it is similar in concept to those at Cheltenham (*Plate 34*), Loughborough (*Plate 195*) and at Melton Mowbray.

Plate 84: A more elevated view of the glass awning of the 'up' platform. The large building protruding through the platform canopy is half-timbered, and embellished by many fancy gables, oriole windows and fancy barge boards.

H. N. Twells

Plate 85: Barton & Walton Station, having been prepared for the arrival of King George V for an unofficial visit to Needwood Hall, the home of Lord Burton. The station building was of a substantial size with the stationmaster's large house flanked by a high steeply-pitched roofed office extension. This roof extends outwards to cover a timber-fronted waiting area. The principle features of this building were repeated at Coleshill (originally known as Forge Mill for Coleshill) situated on the same line to Birmingham.

Plate 84

Plate 85

Plate 86: Repton & Willington. A view looking towards Derby. The facilities here are provided in a assortment of timber buildings of varying ancestry. The hipped roof building on the 'up' platform is comparable with those at Warmley on the Bath branch, but otherwise there is no uniformity in other structures. The small building to the left houses the winding gear for a luggage lift.

Lens of Sutton

Plate 87: Repton & Willington. At road level can be seen what must be the original Birmingham & Derby Junction Railway building. The position of the luggage lift has been moved, in this 1960s view. Also worthy of note is the change from vertical paling to diagonal fencing. The suffix 'Repton' was not added to the title until 1872, in recognition of the public school of that name in the vicinity.

BR/OPC Joint Venture

Plate 88: Derby. The covered cab approach to the main entrance of Derby Station in 1951, showing little change since relocation in 1891 (*see Plate 92*).

BR/OPC Joint Venture

Plate 89: Derby. The southern approaches to Derby on a winter's day, as seen from Holland Road bridge. The London Road Junction signal box was later renewed by a structure placed immediately to the north. To the right is the southern end of the original platform. Opposite the signal box stood the 'O' mile post for the Birmingham line.

Plate 90: An interior view of Derby Station looking north, around 1910. On the left is the original platform, the only platform when the station was opened in 1840 by the North Midland Company. The timber platform to the right became platform 2 during alterations to increase station capacity. Two island platforms were added by the Midland Railway, although the outer face of the second island was outside the confines of the original Stephenson train shed.

Plate 91: Derby, gaily decorated in honour of His Majesty King Edward VII, on the occasion of his visit to Derby in June 1906.

BR/OPC Joint Venture

Plate 92 (left): The frontage of Derby Station, showing parts of the original Francis Thompson building. Alterations in 1856 and 1872 resulted in the building as shown here.

Plate 93 (below): Later alterations included the building of a two storey symmetrical facade, capped with balustrading, extending between three storey pedimented office blocks. Three pediments decorated the frontage, the centre one containing a clock and three Wyverns. The glass-roofed porte-cochère was relocated in front of the new extension to achieve the ultimate form. The 'Arrival' and 'Departure' boards, which appear to be fabricated from standard iron lettering, had been removed by 1925.

Derby to Chesterfield

The preliminary survey carried out by George Stephenson for the North Midland Railway in 1835 to find the best route from Derby to Leeds resulted in a line using river valleys for ease of construction although avoiding Sheffield, Barnsley, and Wakefield. The Act for this line was ratified in February 1847, contracts were let, and work quickly started. Deposits of coal were found whilst excavating Clay Cross Tunnel, these later proving lucrative to George Stephenson and to the Midland Railway.

Francis Thompson was engaged to design the stations, and the fine structure at Wingfield remained in use until passenger services were withdrawn on 2nd Janaury 1967.

The official opening of the line as far as Rotherham took place on 11th May 1840 with the usual pomp and ceremony. The Rotherham to Leeds section opened during the following July.

The North Midland station for Duffield was located some distance to the south of the one depicted here. This station was constructed at the junction of the Wirksworth branch to coincide with its opening on 1st October 1867. In both platform views, the Wirksworth branch platform is behind and to the left of the photographer.

Plate 94: A view from the 'up' platform at Duffield, looking north, prior to the line being widened. Work has obviously started, as the footbridge carrying the public footpath has been installed allowing closure of a level crossing. The signal is pulled off for the main line, and the other signal controls entry to a 'down' loop adjacent to the goods yard.

Plate 95: A scene photographed after the widening at Duffield. The old 'up' platform became the 'down', through which a train has just passed. The erstwhile 'down' platform was rarely used for passengers after widening. The footbridge in the foreground is unusually supported on timber framing, and one suspects that the main girders had previously seen use elsewhere. The footbridge near the signal box is also unusually supported on lattice girder stanchions, another departure from normal Midland practice. No platform was provided on the 'up' goods line.

Plate 96: The Duffield Station building is reminiscent of the structure at King's Norton and Moseley (*Figure 6*), with a similar chimney, round-topped windows and fancy barge boards, some of which unfortunately have had to be replaced with plain boards in this 1969 view. Note the additional chimney pots.

Plate 97: Belper. The North Midland Railway passed Belper in a cutting, and so it sited its station on open ground to the south of the town. This proved to be very inconvenient, so as the Midland Railway were forced to replace the brick support walls of the cutting which were continually bulging at the same time, in 1878, they prepared a new station nearer to the town centre. A pair of gabled twin-pavilioned buildings facing each other from opposite platforms proved sufficient for local needs. The platforms were approached by long ramps from an overbridge, and the main building stood adjacent to the King Street bridge on the west side of the railway.

Plate 98: Dronfield

Plate 99: Dronfield. *Lens of Sutton*

Plate 100: Beauchief and Abbey Dale.

Plate 101: Millhouses and Ecclesall. *Lens of Sutton*

At Tapton Junction we turn off the North Midland line on to a line which was opened in 1870 direct to Sheffield. This city had been avoided in Stephenson's original plan, but subsequently this line became the main passenger route for the Midland Railway to the north, so at last Sheffield was on the main line instead of merely on a branch from Masborough. The three stations illustrated were originally provided with similar hipped roof timber buildings bearing round-topped windows and doorways. These buildings remained in

use at Dronfield until its first closure in 1967 (*Plate 98*), although at some time an extension was added to the right-hand end of the one shown. This type of building is similar to those at Warmley on the Bath extension and was constructed in the same decade. Dronfield experienced a change of footbridge in 1921 when the timber-trussed type, in the earlier view, was replaced by a plate girder bridge on brick piers (*Plate 99*). In consequence of an increase in traffic, the line north of Dore was quadrupled between 1901 and 1903 so the stations received extra facilities accordingly. Beauchief and Millhouses were two stations similarly equipped, each being entered from an overbridge into a tall steeply-roofed half-timbered edifice, giving access by stairway to an island platform on which stood a flat-roofed timber structure with deep valancing. This type of building became a familiar sight during this period when a great deal of new work was being undertaken. We shall see many more examples of this theme during our excursions. *Plate 102* shows Beauchief as it appeared before widening took place.

The changes in title of these two stations is interesting. Beauchief was originally Abbeyhouses, then Beauchief in 1870, Beauchief and Abbey Dale in 1889. Finally it became Beauchief in 1914. Millhouses was originally Ecclesall, then Ecclesall and Millhouses in 1871. Mill House and Ecclesall in 1884, and finally became Millhouses and Ecclesall in 1937.

Plate 102: Beauchief and Abbey Dale before widening.
H. N. Twells Collection

Plate 103: Permanent way almost to perfection. A 1949 view, looking south towards the station, from Dore & Totley Station Junction signal box. The main line to Chesterfield and the south eases to the left, with that to the Hope Valley vanishing beneath the road overbridge immediately beyond the station platforms. The original junction with the Chinley line, previously to the south of the station, was moved northwards to this point around 1903.

BR/OPC Joint Venture

Plate 104: The arrival of the Chinley line at Dore did little to alter the station scene. However, with the widening and station improvements covering a period from 1901 to 1903, Dore & Totley changed considerably. The small brick shelter on the right gave way to a timbered structure with a large flat canopy serving an island platform, produced as a result of the improvements. This late nineteenth century view, looking towards Sheffield, shows once again an earlier type of footbridge similar in design to those at Ashchurch and Berkeley Road, but with a much larger lattice girder. It was replaced in 1903 by another design of lattice (small) girder bridge, erected to connect the existing platforms to the two added on the east side for the widening.

Plate 105: The busy scene is framed by the 1903 footbridge. Passengers are under no illusion that access to the other three platforms is gained by using this facility. The very commercial outlook of the Company is highlighted by the presence of a picture postcard stand alongside a guide rack. Platform 1, from which this picture was taken, served trains from the Hope Valley line.

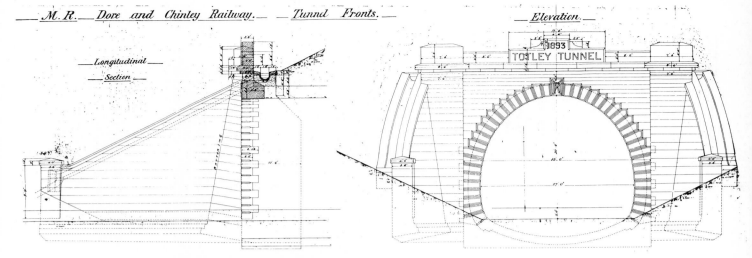

Longitudinal Section

Elevation

1893
TOTLEY TUNNEL

Figure 7: Totley Tunnel. Part of an official drawing of the western entrance.

British Rail

No. 1104. Grindleford Station.

The Dore and Chinley branch, as the Midland Railway identified it, provided the last of the cross-Pennine routes when it opened in 1894.

Construction of the line was expensive, the two tunnels, Totley and Cowburn, accounting for the major proportion of the costs. A large degree of uniformity was apparent in the design of the structures, particularly the stations within the Hope Valley section. An economical eye was cast when assessing the needs of local requirements, resulting in the provision of booking, toiletry and commercial facilities in a single building adjacent to the station entrances. Simple waiting-rooms of almost identical design were provided on the platforms.

Plate 106 (above): The view experienced by passengers from the 'up' platform of Grindleford Station. The western entrance, detailed in *Figure 9,* is behind the three-arched stone overbridge, detailed in *Figure 8.*

Figure 8: A detailed elevation of the road overbridge situated immediately to the west of the tunnel portal.

British Rail

Elevation

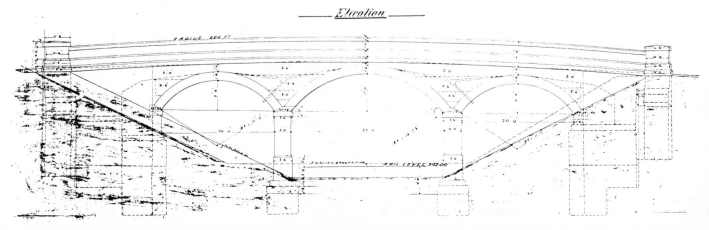

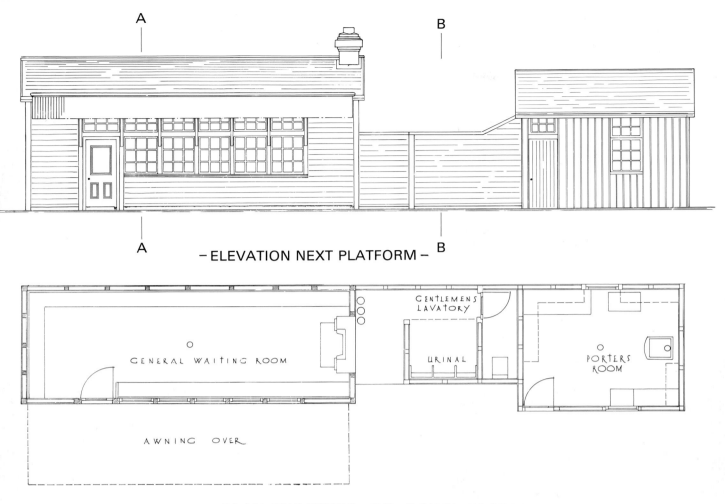

A   B

– ELEVATION NEXT PLATFORM –

A   B

GENERAL WAITING ROOM

GENTLEMENS LAVATORY

URINAL

PORTERS ROOM

AWNING OVER

PLAN-BUILDINGS ON DOWN PLATFORM

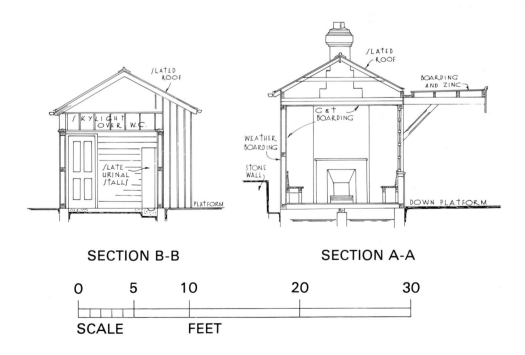

SLATED ROOF

SKYLIGHT OVER W.C.

SLATE URINAL STALLS

PLATFORM

SLATED ROOF

BOARDING AND ZINC

G & t BOARDING

WEATHER BOARDING

STONE WALL

DOWN PLATFORM

SECTION B-B   **SECTION A-A**

0   5   10   20   30

SCALE   FEET

GRINDLEFORD-DOWN SIDE STATION BUILDING

Figure 9: Grindleford. Elevations and plan of the 'down' side buildings, based on a drawing made by the LMS District Engineer (Derby North). The main difference was the timber cladding below window level as compared with the stone at Bamford *(Plate 110)*. The porters' room was not an original feature, but was most certainly a Midland addition.

Plate 108: The heavily wooded hillside above the western entrance of Totley Tunnel dwarfs Grindleford Station. The view belies the station's location on a short embankment through which ran a large culvert. However, this accounts for the timber construction of the platform buildings and a section of the platforms. The platform fencing was, by Midland standards, a most unattractive feature, and was later replaced by the more traditional diagonal type seen on the left. The wooden platforms were themselves replaced by concrete units, probably by the LMS.

Plate 110: Bamford Station platforms were reached by stone steps from the adjacent road overbridge at the Edale end. The booking office was on the 'down' side at road level, and produced in an attractive mixture of dressed stone and timber in a similar manner to the platform buildings. The stationmaster's house to the right was a most desirable residence by any standard, similar buildings being erected at Hathersage and Hope.

Lens of Sutton

Plate 107: A view of the station approach at Grindleford around the turn of the century. The main station building of stone/hall and timber construction is to the left of the picture and housed the booking office/hall and stationmaster's facilities. One can imagine the homeward-bound Sheffield businessmen anticipating a scene such as this. The village was approximately a mile away.

Plate 109: Another station with timber platforms was Hathersage which was provided with a sizeable goods yard and a typical Midland water tank. A passing loop was sited on the 'up' side, presumably to provide relief on the approach to Totley. The moor under which the tunnel is bored is seen in the background in this view looking east from the 'down' platform.

Plate 111: The busiest and most extensive station on the line, Hope (for Castleton and Bradwell) somehow managed to receive different treatment than other D&C stations, as it produced pieces of untypical Midland architecture. Small, all wooden, single storey buildings were provided on each platform and were connected by a robust wrought and cast-iron footbridge which, at the time, was the standard design for spanning two lines of way with platforms (*see A Pictorial Record of LMS Architecture — Figure 59*). Within the decade after opening, Hope Station was further extended by the lengthening of the platforms at the western end, with additional buildings on each side containing general waiting and ladies' rooms. The 'up' platform is illustrated in this view, the original buildings being in the foreground. Of note are the substantial dressed stone copings which varied in lengths of up to 9ft.

Plate 113: Cross-platform interchange for passengers was the main function of Chinley, and it is not surprising that the entrance was rather uninspiring, as seen in this view, and leaving local feelings somewhat aggravated at the need to circumnavigate several flights of stairs.

Plate 112: Edale. With the exception of Hope, arrangements for Edale compared to those considered adequate for the other intermediate stations. The two platform shelters were supplemented by the usual booking office/hall combination on the 'down' side, this time adjacent to a road underbridge at the Hope end of the station. The platforms were connected by a stone arched subway. The end loading dock, in the right foreground, was a feature of many railway stations, not only those on the Midland. The vertical paled fencing was a 'standard' feature, until the more familiar diagonal fencing was adopted as standard in 1909.

Lens of Sutton

Plate 114: Chinley, as a result of the Midland Railway's ambitious plans for the area, acquired a new station some 400yds. west of the original two-platformed site. In this 1903 view looking from the south, Chinley Station South signal box is to the right, with the 'up' slow line platform nearing completion. The station became a major junction for traffic to and from the north-west, retaining its importance until the 1960s, when electrification of the former LNWR lines to Manchester and Liverpool quickly brought about its demise.

BR/OPC Joint Venture

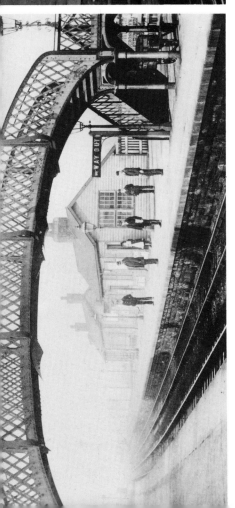

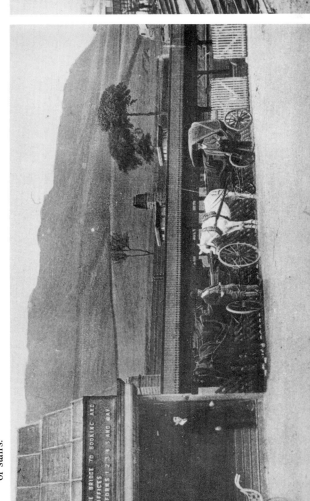

Plate 115: Cheadle Heath. The largest of the stations on the Manchester direct line (New Mills to Heaton Mersey, opened in 1902), was Cheadle Heath, which was strategically located to serve the southern suburbs of Manchester, and provide easier access to the port of Liverpool, via the Cheshire Lines system. A line from Chinley to New Mills opened in 1867 to complete a route from the Midlands towards Manchester. Access to the city involved running via devious routes over other Company's metals, until small lengths of line of its own creation allowed access to the new joint station at Manchester (Central). This well-planned station at Cheadle Heath had features which were probably the ultimate in period station design. The flat cantilevered canopies created large clear areas of platform, appreciated by passengers and railway staff alike. All five platforms were connected by a covered footbridge from a brick built booking office at road level. Extensive goods facilities were provided on the 'down' side, highlighted by a large two storey goods warehouse seen on the left of this 1902 view, looking towards the Manchester direction.

BR/OPC Joint Venture

Plate 117: Heaton Mersey. Forming a junction with the Manchester South District Railway, the Midland Railway regained the 'old' route into Manchester at Heaton Mersey, where the main building had very strong affiliation with stations to be found on the Cheshire Lines system. A small goods yard dealt mainly with coal, for which the Midland Railway provided a steel coal chute in 1902.

Lens of Sutton

Plate 116: Cheadle Heath. This platform level study of Midland station detail at Cheadle Heath illustrates the unexpectedly large proportions of the angled nameboard together with the lamps and water crane. Platform surfacing, away from the main covered area, was unpretentious, perhaps reflecting the irregular use of these platform extremities. Another variation in edging is worth noting when compared to the heavy stone version used in the Hope Valley.

BR/OPC Joint Venture

Plate 118: Withington. The expanse of glazed awnings and screens is well illustrated in this view of Withington (later called Withington & Albert's Park in 1884, and Withington & West Didsbury in 1914). The design for this station was repeated at Didsbury with the approach from road level directly on to the footbridge, platform access being gained by flights of stairs. Details of stations and screen can be fund in *A Pictorial Record of LMS Architecture*. These stations were on the Manchester South District Railway incorporated, in 1873, which was taken into the Midland fold in 1877 and opened in 1880.

Lens of Sutton

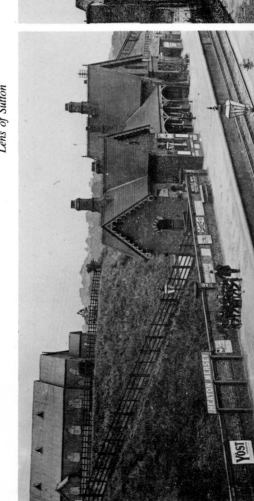

Plate 119: Morecambe Station viewed from the site of the Midland Hotel whilst it enjoys a quiet spell in the summer, some 2½ years after opening. This majestic building was designed by the architect A. Wheatley, under the direction of W. B. Worthington, in keeping with the sea front amenities of the day. The frontage design was a more elaborate form of the building at Northumberland Street which, in its turn, had been copied at Lancaster (Green Ayre). The title 'Promenade' was not added until 1924.

The first tentative bid to bring a railway to the shores of Morecambe Bay was by the Morecambe Bay & Harbour Company for a harbour at, and a connecting line to, Lancaster from Poulton-le-Sands, the village that was the forerunner of the large seaside resort later known as Morecambe. With the title changed to Morecambe Harbour & Railway Company, the Act of Parliament was granted on 16th June 1846, but almost immediately this company united with the new North Western Railway who had received authorisation during the same month. The intention of the latter company was to serve the area west of Skipton by connecting the Leeds & Bradford Railway with the Lancaster & Carlisle Railway.

The section from Lancaster to a station on the jetty of the harbour at Poulton-le-Sands opened on 12th June 1848, and the rest of the line to Skipton opened in stages during 1849 and 1850.

In 1852 the Midland agreed to work the North Western for a period of 21 years, but on 1st January 1859 were granted a 999 year lease, finally absorbing the Company some 13 years later, on 1st July 1871.

At Poulton-le-Sands in 1851, a timber station was constructed at Northumberland Street to serve the town. This was replaced in 1872 by an excellent stone structure, with a train shed over the two running lines.

The Promenade Station was constructed at a time of expansion, the town having by then become well-established as a seaside resort. Providing facilities far in excess of those previously experienced, the new station opened on 24th March 1907, replacing the cramped premises of Northumberland Street. Built by Coates, Murgatroyd & Sons of Bradford to a design of A. Wheatley, a large circulating area was fronted by a mild Gothic frontage executed in light coloured stone. Reputedly planned on similar lines to Bradford, (Forster Square), there were four platforms, each of 250yds., in addition to the extensive carriage sidings.

continued from previous page

Mention must be made of the substantial numbers visiting Morecambe in the holiday season, which was extended to October by the well-known illuminations. A traffic report for 1937 showed that a total of 507 special trains arrived in the town, 265 at Promenade Station, and 242 at the nearby Euston Road. Some 202,669 passengers were handled at Promenade Station, illustrating the heavy demands on facilities.

M.R. MORECAMBE.

──── NEW STATION. ────

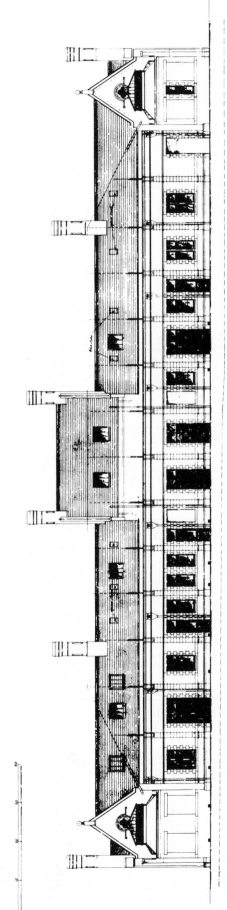

ELEVATION TO CIRCULATING AREA.

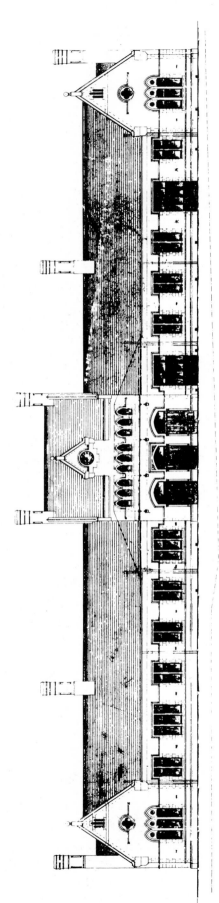

FRONT ELEVATION.

Figure 10: Elevations of the front and circulating area, taken from an official drawing.

Plate 120: Morecambe Promenade. The spacious glass-roofed circulating area in July 1907. A view to be compared with the elevation shown in *Figure 10.*

M.R. MORECAMBE

Figure 11: Further elevations of the main station building. The three entrances in the circulating area elevation give access to the platforms. The contractor's signature can be seen on the right, above that of the architect. All sections of the drawing are from an official drawing.

British Rail

— NEW STATION —

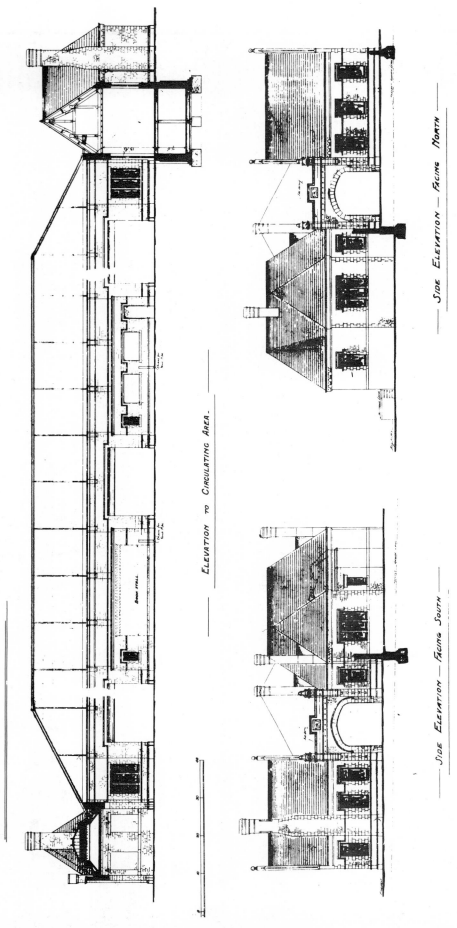

— ELEVATION TO CIRCULATING AREA —

— SIDE ELEVATION — FACING SOUTH —

— SIDE ELEVATION — FACING NORTH —

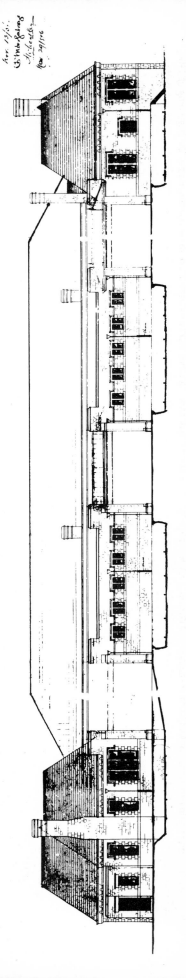

distance to the right of the signal box. The Midland had announced electrification plans in 1906, to enable them to gain experience of that form of traction and operation. The relatively isolated Lancaster-Morecambe-Heysham section was chosen. On 13th April 1908, services started between Morecambe and Heysham, and those to Lancaster in June, using a 6,600 volt overhead system, with electricity generated at a power-station which had been built at Heysham to operate equipment at the harbour. Subsequently, the town supply and later the National Grid was used as a source of power. By 1950, wear and tear caused by the frequent

electric traction started in 1953 using converted Willesden to Earl's Court stock. Except for a short break from October 1955 to March 1956, these continued until the beginning of 1966, when this and the line to Wennington were closed. This view clearly shows the types of structure used to support the contact wires for overhead collection. Over normal double track, a steel girder was supported on wooden poles, but for large spans steel lattice was employed. The site of the Northumberland Street Station is to the right of the picture.

Lancaster

Plate 122: Greyhound Viaduct, Lancaster, October 1907. A view showing the second bridge provided to carry trains across the River Lune on their way between Lancaster and Morecambe. The original, a timber structure erected in 1848, was replaced in 1864 by this bridge which was situated immediately to the north. Wrought-iron lattice girders, cross girders and rail bearers were supported on eight rows of cast-iron screwed piles and bracing. The single line up to Lancaster Castle Station, opened in 1849, is hidden behind the bridge, but its route is to the front of the warehouses.

Plate 123: Greyhound Viaduct, Lancaster, March 1911. A third and final bridge was deemed necessary following increased traffic and electrification. Work on the replacement, which was on a similar alignment to the 1848 bridge, proceeded steadily with completion taking place towards the end of 1911. The increased radius of curvature resulted in longer spans, although still eight in number. Pairs of concrete-filled steel cylinders supported steel main girders and cross girders. This view shows work in progress. Lancaster (Green Ayre) Station is to the right. This station was built by the Midland Railway in 1871 to replace the North Western structure.

Plate 124: Greyhound Viaduct, Lancaster, in February 1912 after the completion of the new viaduct. The view actually gives a clearer picture of the respective locations of the structures, the older overhead catenary in the background indicating the route of the branch to Lancaster (Castle) Station. Demolition of the 1864 viaduct is in its final stages in this view which should be compared with *Plate 122.* The bridge was numbered 134 on the Skipton to Morecambe line, and is now converted for use by road vehicles.

Plate 125: Lancaster. This structure and the footbridge in the distance were provided to serve the workmen's station for a munitions factory at Lancaster in 1916. One suspects that the main girders had been used elsewhere prior to installation on this site, but the construction of the timber piers and steps reflects the temporary nature of the structure. The bridges were removed in 1924.

M.R. TORRISHOLME.

PROPOSED WORKMEN'S PLATFORM.

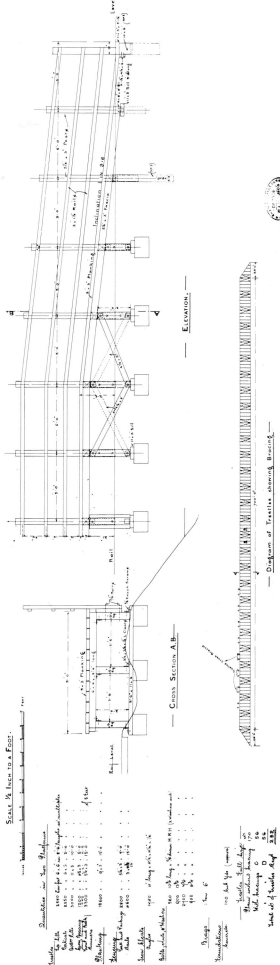

Figure 12: During the period of World War I many platforms of a temporary nature were erected throughout the country to serve factories involved in the war effort. The example here illustrates a lightweight trestle type provided at Torrisholme, near Morecambe, in 1916.

Plate 126

Plate 127

Carlisle to Settle Junction

The LMS Sectional Appendix (1931) to the working timetables simply gives details appertaining to the Durran Hill Sidings to Skipton (South Junction) section of the Midland Division. This somewhat disguises the fact that the 72 miles to Settle Junction contains that magnificently engineered railway — the Settle & Carlisle.

Founded by a desire to have control of its own route to Scotland in the face of problems encountered at the hands of the LNWR, the Midland Railway sought to construct its own railway between Settle and Carlisle as a result of an Act of Parliament dated 16th July 1866. Authorisation empowered the Company to construct the railway in three parts, from a junction with the 'little' North Western Railway's Skipton and Morecombe line, near Settle, to Carlisle, by means of a junction with the NER at Petterill Bridge.

The cost of £3½ million reflected the magnitude of the operation which, in taking some seven years, witnessed the construction of numerous monumental undertakings including some 20 viaducts, 14 tunnels, and a multitude of smaller structures carrying and crossing the line. Generally acknowledged as one of the greatest achievements in the history of English railway construction, the Engineer responsible was J. S. Crossley, long standing Chief Engineer to the Company. Due to retire as work on the line neared completion, Crossley was retained as consultant and the way and works remain as a tribute and fitting memorial to his work for the Midland Railway.

With only minor variations, the stations shared a high degree of uniformity, using a style evolved by Crossley to create a single storey building with gabled pavilions for all but two of the stations.

Despite all the difficulties, the Settle to Carlisle line opened for business on 2nd August 1875.

Plate 126: Scotby. The first of the intermediate stations out from Carlisle, Scotby, had the unique distinction of being the most northerly of the Midland system. The twin-gabled main building was of a style familiar not only to the Settle to Carlisle line, but elsewhere on the network. Scotby was one of eight stations constructed by Messrs G. Black of Carlisle. One unusual feature was the wooden shelter on the left, a type which was not repeated on the route.

Lens of Sutton

Plate 127: Armathwaite. With the exception of Hawes Junction and Culgarth, three basic designs, numbered 1 (large), 2 (medium) and 3 (small) were adopted for the station. Armathwaite, like Scotby, was of No. 2 design. The small shelter opposite was also of a basic design found in brick, stone or timber at other locations.

Plate 128: Lazonby. Uniformity was not only confined to stations. Goods sheds were similarly treated, as this 1913 view at Lazonby illustrates. The standard Midland loading gauge at the entrance to the shed was also a Settle to Carlisle feature.

Plate 128

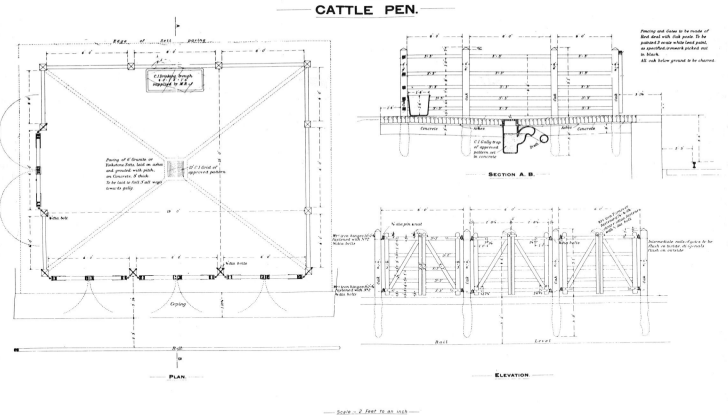

MIDLAND RAILWAY.

CATTLE PEN.

Figure 13: A part drawing of a 'standard' Midland Railway cattle pen.

Plate 129: The extensive provision of cattle facilities at Lazonby highlights the importance of the traffic to the rural communities. Although this design of pen was specifically intended for the Settle & Carlisle, the features are strongly related to the standard drawing detailed in *Figure 13*.

D. Jenkinson

Plate 130: Continuing south, the station at Culgaith, which was not opened until 1880, was located adjacent to a small crossing, shown on early Midland Railway plans, with a gatehouse. It is not evident what type of gates were used or what status the crossing enjoyed, but proposals for the new station included substantial earthworks, roads, signals and gates. Use was made of the gatehouse which formed the central section of the main building. An extension to the left was to be a waiting shed, and the other end, the booking office. Platforms, buildings and a weighing machine brought the estimated cost of the new station to £3,601. In the event, an additional building, shown in this view, was constructed at platform level.

Plate 131: A view of Long Marton as seen from the 'down' platform, looking towards Carlisle. The main buildings are of the medium (No. 2 design) size, but this time executed in brick. The fretted barge boarding is again very much in evidence.

Lens of Sutton

Plate 132: Appleby, as one of the more populated settlements on the route, was provided with the larger type (No. 1 design) of main building. The distinctive twin-pavilioned style received a third but smaller gable to the left-hand end (see platform elevation, *Figure 14*). Again the buildings were of brick with stone detail. This view is photographed from the footbridge, looking south.

Lens of Sutton

M.R.
SETTLE TO CARLISLE
STATION BUILDINGS Nº I AT SETTLE AND KIRKBY STEPHEN

0   5   10   20
SCALE   FEET

ELEVATION OF PORTION OF BUILDING NEXT PLATFORM

Figure 14: A drawing based on an original, giving details of the No. 1 (large) design for stations at Appleby, Kirkby Stephen and Settle.

Plate 133: Appleby, showing screen detail to the 'waiting shed' of the main building (*see Figure 14*).

D. Jenkinson

Plate 134: Ormside Station was rather remote
fact it was not considered when the original lis
stations was drawn up. However, in this view,
prominent features include the stationmaster's h
to the left, with staff cottages, of which two w
provided, to the right. Rear views of station buildi
are infrequent, so it is pertinent to note the si
gable end extension of the small, or No. 3 des
station provided on the line.

Lens of Su

Plate 135: Crosby Garrett was unusually placed
cutting with sizeable retaining walls. The
station building shown here was at the norther
Carlisle end of the 'up' platform, and was of
medium No. 2 design. The house to the left was
for the stationmaster. Both Ormside and Cr
Garrett were closed to all traffic in 1952.

Plate 136: A view of Kirkby Stephen, loo
towards Carlisle. The station was badly placed for
town, but still warranted the larger No. 1 typ
station building, similar to Appleby and Settle
stone version of the small waiting shelter can be
opposite.

Lens of Su

Plate 137: Hawes Junction, renamed H
Junction & Garsdale in 1900, is shown prior t
replacement of the North and South signal boxe
1910 by one situated nearer the waiting shelter o
left. The platform for Hawes and the NER bran
Northallerton is to the right of the island platf

Plate 138: Dent, Ribblehead and Horton-in-Ribblesdale were all similar in design. The former was some four miles from the village which it served, but facilities were consistent with the other small stations on the line. This view of Dent Station looking towards Settle, again illustrates the stone waiting shelter and 'small' size main building.

Plate 139: Ribblehead, originally intended as Ingleton Road, lies in a notoriously bleak spot, and for some time had numerous examples of meteorological equipment to record the extreme conditions. The booking hall housed an organ for the occasional religious service. Looking south, this view again illustrates the smaller type of building as does the view of Horton-in-Ribblesdale.

Plate 140: Horton-in-Ribblesdale, but this time looked at from the opposite direction.

Plate 141: Settle was of the large No. 1 design stations like Appleby and Kirkby Stephen. This view shows the main building placed on the 'up' platform.

D. Jenkinson

Plate 142: Bell Busk looking to the east. The building typifies those produced by the North Western Railway in the mock Tudor appearance of timber and plaster, a style repeated elsewhere on the line, with individual variations of layout and accommodation.

Lens of Sutton

Plate 143: A Midland station scene at Bell Busk around the turn of the century. Note the Midland platform seat.

MIDLAND RAILWAY.

FOOTBRIDGE AT BELL BUSK STATION.

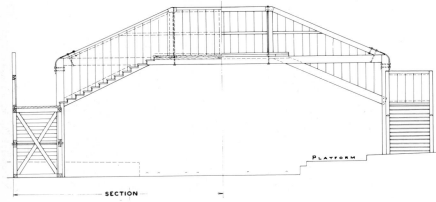

SECTION

ELEVATION.

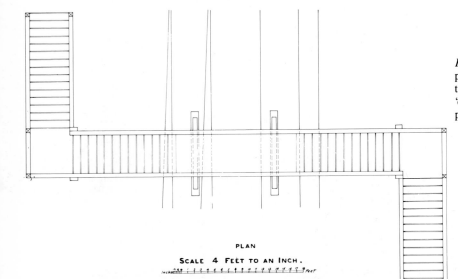

PLAN

SCALE 4 FEET TO AN INCH.

Figure 15: To replace two sleeper level crossings between the staggered platforms at Bell Busk, a footbridge was erected in 1888 at an estimated cost of £155 (Way & Works Committee Minute No. 8655).The most unusual aspect was the choice of timber, at a time when the Midland Railway had established the practice of the use of wrought-iron lattice types for spanning two tracks. A bridge comprising timber-trussed beams, trestles and stepways, was provided at the Settle end of the station. The drawing is based on 1922 information.

The Little North Western

Bell Busk stood on the original main line of the North Western Railway. The prefix 'little' was often added to the title 'North Western' to avoid confusion with the company running the West Coast Main Line. This was to run from Skipton through to the Lancaster & Carlisle Railway, near Tebay. The section north of Ingleton was abandoned by the North Western Railway in favour of the branch from Clapham to Lancaster. The line from Skipton to Ingleton opened in 1849, but within a year, the Clapham to Ingleton portion closed and did not reopen until the line from Ingleton to Lowgill was built in 1861 by the Lancaster & Carlisle Railway, by then part of the LNWR, empowered under the Lancaster & Carlisle & Ingleton Railway Act of 25th August 1857. At the same time, another Act permitted the North Western Railway to abandon its authorised line north of Ingleton, and also to lease or sell the whole railway to the Midland.

Plate 144: Bell Busk, showing the 1888 timber footbridge. The position of the staggered platforms can also be seen. One of the timber crossings replaced by the footbridge was at the left-hand 'down' platform, the other crossed from the end of the 'up' platform to a waiting shelter opposite.

L&GRP, Courtesy David & Charles

Bingley

Bingley was the recipient of a 'temporary' station when the Shipley & Colne extension of the Leeds & Bradford Railway opened in 1847. *Plate 145* shows this station on the last day of use in 1892. Obviously this proved inadequate, for in 1889, the Midland Traffic Committee decided that a new station was called for. This was built south of the overbridge on the opposite side to the original and opened at 6a.m. on 24th July 1892. To a design of Charles Trubshaw, it was constructed in light coloured stone with many embellishments, including stone ball decorations. (*Plates 147 and 148*). As the station was in a cutting next to Bingley Tunnel, the main entrance at road level led on to a passenger overbridge, with wide stairways leading to the platforms. Ridge and furrow awnings were lavishly provided, not only over both platforms (*Plates 146 and 147*) but as passenger protection at the entrance and over the parcels area (*Plate 148*). These were executed in the Midland Railway's final style, using rolled section beams supported on the minimum of slender cast columns, with little decoration.

Plate 145: Bingley Old Station.

Plate 146: Bingley Station. *Lens of Sutton*

Plate 147: Bingley, 1981.

Plate 148: Bingley Station exterior, May 1957. *G. J. Biddle*

Plate 149: Apperley Bridge & Rawdon.

Plate 150: Calverley & Rodley, looking towards Leeds.

Plate 151: Newlay & Horsforth.

The Leeds & Bradford Railway

Parties had strived for a railway from Bradford to Leeds from 1832. However, it was not until 4th July 1844 that an Act received Royal Assent, incorporating the Leeds & Bradford Railway for a line to run from Leeds along the Aire Valley to Shipley, and then to Bradford, with connections at Leeds to the North Midland Railway. There were also provisions for the line to be sold or leased to the North Midland Company. A further Act of June 1845 allowed an extension through Skipton to Colne.

Robert Stephenson had been asked to do a survey, and was appointed Principal Engineer, with F. M. Young as his assistant, and S. D. Martin to do survey work. Thomas Gooch, another Stephenson associate, became responsible for the Skipton & Colne extension (T. L. Gooch was the elder brother of the GWR's Daniel Gooch).

Overtures from other companies and offers of a merger with the Manchester & Leeds Company caused much dismay to the Midland Railway, but in August 1846, the Leeds & Bradford Railway was leased to the Midland Railway for 999 years. An Act of 24th July 1851 allowed the Midland Railway to purchase the L&BR.

After the official inaugural run on Tuesday, 30th June, public services commenced on Wednesday, 1st July 1846, but freight services did not start until September. At the time of opening, a single platform sufficed at Leeds, and none of the intermediate stations were in use. It was two months before wooden island platforms were in use at Shipley, Calverley, Newlay and Kirkstall. Early in 1847, Apperley Bridge Station was being built with outside platforms, and work started on replacing the others.

From the opening of the Leeds & Bradford terminus at Leeds (Wellington), Midland passenger trains ceased to use the Hunslet Lane terminus and instead were accommodated at Leeds (Wellington). However Wellington Station was not finally completed until late in 1849. Hunslet Lane became a goods station.

The Skipton & Colne extension from Shipley opened in stages. On 16th March 1847, public services commenced to a temporary station at Keighley. In September of the same year, Skipton was reached, but again to a temporary station. It was not until October 1848 that trains ran to Colne, although the connection with the East Lancashire railway was not completed through from Burnley until February 1849.

These illustrations show the stations after the extensive widening between Leeds and Shipley at the turn of the century. The alignment of the 1846 route was altered in various ways to accommodate the new works. Work commenced between Apperley Bridge and Calverley in 1896. A second tunnel at Thackley was brought into use in 1901 coinciding with the opening of the widened section from Guiseley Junction, near Shipley, to Apperley. The remaining sections through Newlay & Horsforth and Kirkstall to Leeds followed in 1904 and 1906 respectively. All the widened stations were provided with road-level booking offices, either on or adjacent to the road overbridge, replacing facilities originally provided at platform level. At Apperley Bridge & Rawdon (*Plate 149*) the widening was to the left of this view which looks towards Shipley. The new 'down' slow platform received the benefit of a ridge and furrow awning on the platform building. The wide island had an extensive flat-roofed structure, somewhat similar to the ones we have seen at Beauchief and Millhouses. At Calverley & Rodley, a road overbridge was constructed between 1875 and 1877 to replace a level crossing. The bridge was extended for the 1901 widening, and received a half-timbered building with herringbone detail. Here and at Newlay & Horsforth (*Plate 151*), gabled pavilion type structures had been provided in the 1870s. These had basic similarities to the ones seen at Moseley and King's Norton. The island platforms at Calverley and at Newlay were quite narrow, and only received centrally supported flat-roofed canopies. The waiting shelter, seen on the left, at Calverley, was an attractive timber/brick structure of unusual design. The overbridge at Newlay & Horsforth (*Plate 151*) was constructed in 1881, again replacing a level crossing. It was extended over the slow lines in 1904.

Plate 152: The Leeds & Bradford Company station at Kirkstall Forge was closed in 1903 as a result of widening and diversion work. A new station called Kirkstall opened on 7th July 1905. Although contemporary with the other widened stations, it was built to a slightly superior standard. The passenger entrance led into a booking hall set at road level adjacent to an overbridge, which had been reconstructed and an additional span provided in 1905. A footbridge led on to the platforms. This view was photographed shortly after completion in September 1906. Note the platform seat with a high back to act as a windbreak. These were also provided under the canopies at Calverley and at Newlay & Horsforth.

The tram and railways of Leeds intersected on a number of locations. One particular location was Wellington Road, conveniently placed for the Geldard Street entrance to Holbeck Station, opened in 1862. By 1908, there were four separate bridges over each road, three belonging to the Midland Railway and one to the North Eastern, numbered in a conventional but somewhat confusing manner. It seemed quite straightforward to identify the structures as Wellington Road spans 1, 2 and 3 and Geldard Street in a similar way, but the Engineering Department obviously required further clarification by numbering the bridges 16a, 16, 17 and 14a, 14 and 15 respectively.

Plate 153: The tramways along Wellington Road first passed under the North Eastern Railway side of the bridge, the abutment of which was shared with bridge No. 17 on the Midland line. This was the scene in August 1915, prior to commencement of work involved in the reconstruction of bridges Nos. 15 and 17.

Plate 154: A view on top of the bridge, also in August 1915, looking along the 'up' and 'down' fast lines towards Armley, with the North Eastern lines to Harrogate on the right. This is the alignment for the original route, a wrought-iron structure of 1890 replacing the 1846 bridge. Over the next few months, larger girders of steel would provide a replacement for future road widening schemes.

Plate 156: The last bridge to be constructed over Geldard Street was No. 14a, pictured here, carrying sidings for the gasworks opened at Holbeck in 1909. Completed in 1908, using steel, the details are similar to those used for the 1915/16 reconstruction of bridges Nos. 15 and 17. This view clearly shows the street level entrance to Holbeck Station.

Plate 155: The completed bridge in May 1916. The signals to the left are for the slow lines and controlled from Westley Junction signal box, which can be seen behind the fast line signals in *Plate 154*. The North Eastern Railway had also seen fit to improve its signalling by providing a gantry being controlled from Geldard Junction signal box. Compare this view with that in *Plate 154*.

Plate 1??. To enable the reconstruction work to be carried out with minimal disruption, interlacing of the tracks was introduced, and can be clearly seen in this view. This method of operation, although causing some delay to train movements, was a feature of Midland practice. It allowed a form of single line working with minimum alterations to track and signalling. The signal at this end of Holbeck Station platform was temporary for the duration of the works. By October, girders on one side of the bridges were in position, only deck waterproofing and reinstatement of permanent way being required. The high-level structure in the background outlines Holbeck (High Level) Station on the Great Northern Railway route to and from Leeds (Central) as it passes over the Midland (Low Level) Station.

104 HOLBECK OCT. 5 1915

Plate 158: A view of Woodlesford, looking towards Leeds. An all embracing view of one of the original North Midland stations, taken at the time when one of the arches of bridge No. 28 (York Road) was reconstructed. Half of the original North Midland Railway's stone parapet has been dismantled, temporary wooden fencing having taken its place. The goods yard on the left has been temporarily taken over by the Engineer's Department. Notice the staggered platforms to the station, and how the 'up' platform on the right has been raised to accommodate track lifting.

Plate 159: The view at road level, looking through the reconstructed arch towards York (later to become the A642). The new brick would have replaced stone, similar to the smaller arch on the right. Incidentally, this smaller arch was private.

South of Leeds

Heading south from Leeds, we are once again on the course of the North Midland Railway discussed earlier, although much of the line was greatly altered from that envisaged by George Stephenson in 1840. Stretches of the line through to Sheffield were widened to four track to help the flow of the greater traffic. Powers for widening had been obtained for the Holbeck area in 1891, whilst new work on much of the line to the south was covered in the Midland Railway Act of 1st July 1898. Work was still being carried out at the time of the Grouping, the tunnel at Chevet then being removed in favour of a very deep cutting to accommodate the four tracks.

Plate 160: A view of Altofts & Whitwood, looking north. A station that has obviously suffered from subsidence, there is evidence of the platforms having been raised to correct levels. Heavy props have had to be provided for the large nameboard. The building on the left does not seem to have affiliations with other structures on the Midland Railway, although the simple shelter on the 'up' side is familiar. This station was opened in 1870.

Plate 161: Sandal and Walton. The station building appears to have traces of North Midland origin, but this is belied by the fact that it did not open until 1870. Use of the signal box was discontinued in 1926, when the LMS continued the widening schemes commenced by the Midland Railway.

Plate 162: An LMS view of Royston & Notton Station, looking north from the signal box. This was on part of the line widened by the Midland Railway in 1900, and replaced an earlier station situated one mile to the north. The fast lines are to the left, and the slow ones to the right. The station layout is typical of Midland practice at enlarged locations, with timber buildings with large flat canopies. The platforms are connected by a subway, and the booking offices are provided at road level. Much Midland Railway 'furniture' is in evidence in the foreground, including a fogman's timber hut between the running lines, corrugated lamp hut, and wooden toilet for the signalman.

BR/OPC Joint Venture

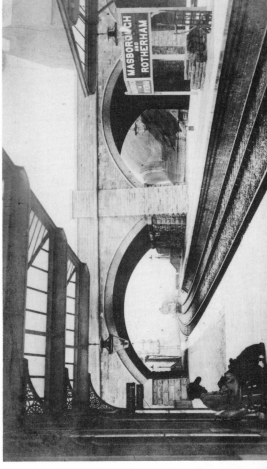

Plate 163: Cudworth was the North Midland Railway's station for Barnsley until the Midland opened a branch to that town in 1870. The station was at first known as Barnsley, but the name Cudworth seems to have been in use since 1854. The North Midland Railway had equipped the station with a building designed by Francis Thompson. This was ultimately replaced, the Midland Railway providing an excellent example of their latter day architecture. This was a plain brick building functional in character but devoid of embellishment. The main building to the left of the picture exhibited a ridge and furrow awning of the final design, using heavy tapered steel joists cantilevered from the station wall, similar to those on the outer platforms at Leicester. The island platform again has the flat-canopied buildings which were becoming so familiar. It is possible to see the roof lights on top of the canopy. A Midland item not yet portrayed in this volume is the oval-shaped platform number. One is seen hanging from the left-hand awning, and two more can be seen adjacent to the footbridge stairway.

Plate 164: Parkgate and Rawmarsh. A view towards Normanton of another widened station. The building on the right is of similar construction to the one on the island, but has a much reduced canopy. The footbridge type was unusual. Before 1869 this station was known as Rawmarsh.

Plate 165: Rotherham. An exterior view in 1970, shortly after refurbishing by British Rail, highlighting the combination of brick and stone with ball finials on the gables, curved arches and windows, the same genre as that seen at Bingley and Castle Bromwich, and also at Cricklewood and Kettering (*see later*), and at Wigston and Coalville.

Plate 166: The completed bridge works and extended platforms following the widening through Masborough & Rotherham in 1903. Compare this view with that in *Plate 167*. The buttressed pier seen on the right centre between the arches is that in the centre of the earlier view. Note the decorated brackets supporting the beams of the ridge and furrow awning. The station opened as Masborough in 1840, was renamed Masborough & Rotherham on 1st May 1896, later became Rotherham (Masborough) in 1908, and British Rail decided to call it Rotherham in 1969.
Lens of Sutton

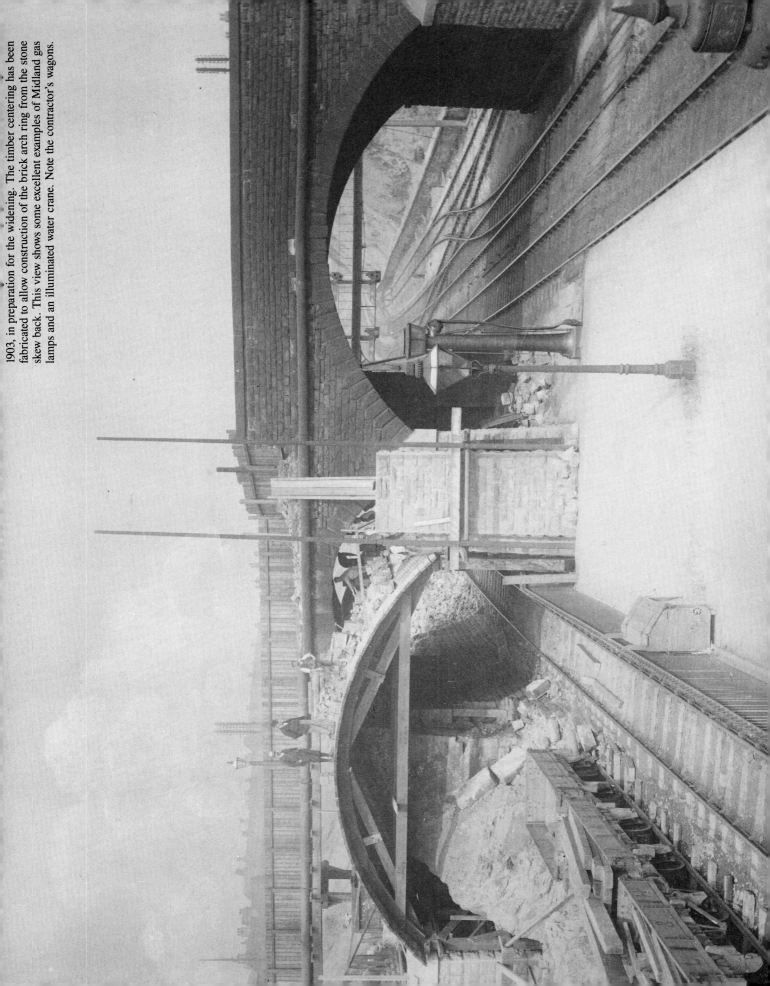

1903, in preparation for the widening. The timber centering has been fabricated to allow construction of the brick arch ring from the stone skew back. This view shows some excellent examples of Midland gas lamps and an illuminated water crane. Note the contractor's wagons.

Plate 168: Mansfield Woodhouse. This was another type of pavilioned building, executed in timber with a low hipped roof embellished with numerous elegant eaves brackets and cocks comb ridge tiling. The recess between the pavilions is effectively shielded from the elements by a glazed screen between cast columns. The whole can be compared with the brick example at Camp Hill, and is of a similar ground plan to that at Blackwell, and to the small stations on the Settle to Carlisle line.

Plate 169: Mansfield. A view looking across the viaduct towards Worksop in 1915. Apart from a change to upper quadrant signalling, the scene changed little into BR times.

Rotherham to Nottingham

South from Masborough towards Nottingham, we must detour over byways built to serve one of the principal coal producing areas of the country. We leave the North Midland main line at Staveley to pass over the branch to Elmton & Cresswell, in order to reach the line from Mansfield to Worksop which opened in 1875. Passing en route through Langwith and Shirebrook, with stations similar to those on the Settle to Carlisle section, we come to Mansfield Woodhouse (*Plate 168*). We proceed to Mansfield which is entered over a 15 arch stone viaduct to a station built for the opening of the Worksop line, replacing the terminal station of 9th October 1849.

Railways had come to Mansfield when the Mansfield and Pinxton line opened on 13th April 1819 as a tramroad, to carry coal to the Cromford Canal at Pinxton. The Midland Railway were authorised to utilise this tramroad as part of their branch from Nottingham to Mansfield by Act of Parliament of 8th July 1847. The line opened on 2nd October 1848 from Nottingham as far as Kirkby in Ashfield. The reconstructed line into Mansfield was not in operation for another year although for some time passengers were carried on the tramway in horse-drawn coaches.

Plate 170: Mansfield. The Midland extol the virtues of 'The Best Route' on the extensive hoarding under the viaduct at the foot of the road approach to the station. The train shed over the platforms can be seen to the right as can the end of the signal gantry seen in *Plate 169*.

Plate 171: Mansfield enjoyed extensive covered facilities in the form of an iron and glass pitched roof over two of its three platforms.

H. C. Casserley

Plate 172: The excessively decorated stone building shown here and in *Plate 171* possibly reflects the importance the Midland Railway attached to the town, in spite of the limited capacity of the station.

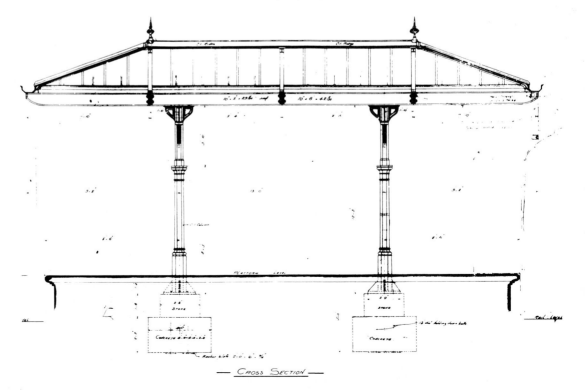

Figure 16: A cross-section, typical of the type of ridge and furrow awning placed on island platform situations at about the turn of the century, and similar to the one used at Mansfield seen on the right in *Plate 171*.

— CROSS SECTION —

Plate 173: An evocative suburban scene at Basford in 1919. The footbridge again follows the pattern seen at Berkeley Road and Ashchurch, but in this case forms a right of way for pedestrians to cross the line should the gates of the Nottingham Road crossing be closed against them. Passengers could use the sleeper crossing.

Compare the dark and light painting of the doors with those at Berkeley Road; these were chocolate (Midland Venetian red) and cream (Midland Denby Pottery). These colours were used on station and goods sheds, but in addition, window glazing bars would be white, and doors to offices and other station amenities were usually maroon with black ironwork.

Nottingham

Plate 175: Carrington Road entrance, Nottingham, shortly after its opening in 1904. The left-hand opening is detailed in *Figure 17*.

The original Midland Counties Railway terminal station at Nottingham opened formally on Thursday, 30th May 1839 on the west side of the then Queen's Road, later called Carrington Street. This remained in use until 1847, when accommodation for the new line to Lincoln was required. A new through station was commenced on the east side of Queen's Road with two 600ft. platforms and four lines between. The station building, facing Station Street, was constructed in a classical style, with six stone columns to the portico.

Further improvements and accommodation were required by 1900 when the present station was started. To a design of Mr A. E. Lambert, a local architect working with the Midland Railway's Engineer Mr J. A. MacDonald, construction was completed in two years. Six platforms with a total length of 5,940ft. were provided. At the Leicester end, an enclosed footbridge with stepways from the platforms gave access to the high-level building facing Carrington Street with its booking offices, large cab approach and concourse.

The improvements at Nottingham continued a pattern set at Leicester and Sheffield. Here, red sandstone, decorated with reddish-brown terracotta, was used to produced pedimented rusticated window openings and carriage entrances to the screen of the large cab approach. A square rusticated clock tower was centrally placed.

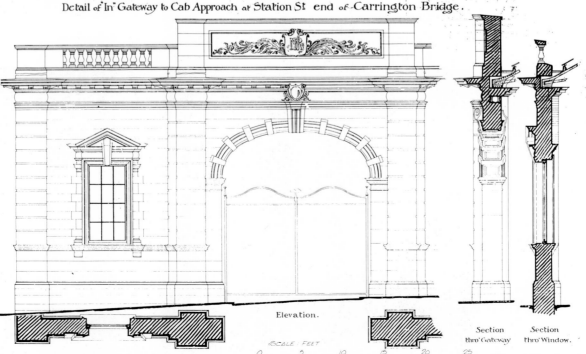

M.R. Nottingham, New Station. Booking Hall Block.
Detail of In Gateway to Cab Approach at Station St end of Carrington Bridge.

Elevation.

SCALE · FEET

Plan

Section thro' Gateway   Section thro' Window.

Figure 17: An elevation from an official drawing

Plate 176: Nottingham. A view beneath the extensive glazed arcade of the cab approach in 1904. Passengers passed through the smaller doorway into the booking hall illustrated in *Figure 18 & Plate 177 (below)*.

M.R. Nottingham, New Station.   Booking Hall Block

Half Longitudinal Section thro' Booking Hall,
(looking towards Booking Office.)

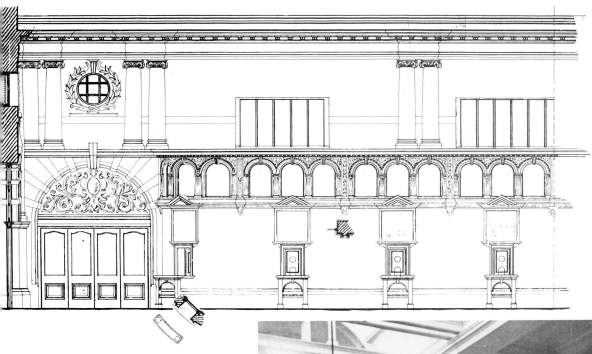

Figure 18: An elevation from an official drawing.

Plate 177: Nottingham. The booking clerks enjoy a quiet spell at Nottingham in 1904.

Plate 178: Nottingham. The platforms are numbered with temporary signs during a period when finishing touches were being applied to the new station, which formally opened on 17th January 1904. Of interest is the cladding to the sides of the large footbridge. This was a feature employed at many stations during this period.

Plate 179: Nottingham. This view looking east shows the bow string girder bridge of the Great Central Railway's London extension, and how it dominates the scene as it crosses the Midland Station a few yards from the Carrington Street entrance.

Plate 180: The Station Street entrance of the 1847 Midland Station at Nottingham, photographed in 1903 at the time of construction work on the new station.

Plate 181: The Nottingham to Lincoln line was one of two mentioned in the introduction, being authorised shortly after formation of the Midland Railway, but obviously planned by the Midland Counties Railway prior to amalgamation. The line opened in August 1846. A number of pretty cottage-style stations resulted. This view shows Burton Joyce, looking west, in June 1903, a small wayside station full of Midland character. The station building has the appearance of a gatehouse and, in fact, has been extended towards the level crossing. Unusual but attractive features are the porched entrance beneath the main gable, and the 'curly' barge boards, somewhat different to the norm. The heavy stone platform copings, previously seen on the Hope Valley line, are in evidence again. Many of these features were repeated at other stations on the line, particularly at Carlton and Netherfield. The signal box is of the early Midland style, displaying 'short' windows all round. Further details on this subject can be found in *A Pictorial Record of LMS Architecture.*

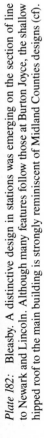

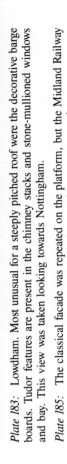

Plate 182: Bleasby. A distinctive design in stations was emerging on the section of line to Newark and Lincoln. Although many features follow those at Burton Joyce, the shallow hipped roof to the main building is strongly reminiscent of Midland Counties designs (cf).

Plate 184: Newark. A subdued classical facade was produced for Newark, with square stone pilasters to the entrance bay and stone window hoods on moulded brackets.

R. J. Essery

Plate 183: Lowdham. Most unusual for a steeply pitched roof were the decorative barge boards. Tudor features are present in the chimney stacks and stone-mullioned windows and bay. This view was taken looking towards Nottingham.

Plate 185: The classical facade was repeated on the platform, but the Midland Railway uncharacteristically managed to hide the elegance in an attempt to improve passenger amenities.

Lens of Sutton

Plate 187

Plate 186: Collingham. East of Newark, stations of Italianate appearance were conceived, varying in style and size. Collingham and Swinderby were similar, having tall buildings with shallow pitched roofs, many chimney stacks and numerous round-topped windows.

R. J. Essery

Plate 187: Swinderby, at some time, received a cross-gable waiting shelter with the well-known lozenge pane windows.

H. C. Casserley

Plate 188: Hykeham was provided with a small single storey building, overshadowed by a massive chimney.

R. J. Essery

Plate 189: Lincoln, at the end of the line from Nottingham, had a frontage truly echoing the symmetrical look of the Station Street building. Ionic columns formed a central portico, and square pilasters adorned the end blocks. Window hoods and brackets were similar to those at Newark. Originally, a stone parapet topped the frontage, but this had to be replaced by brick.

Mowat Collection

Plate 190: The platform at Lincoln received a more fitting pitched train shed with slatted gables.

H. C. Casserley

Plate 190

Plate 186

Plate 188

Plate 189

Plate 191: Kegworth. Little remains of the Midland Counties original facilities in the resultant collection of buildings. In this view, looking towards Leicester, the goods lines of this four track section from Leicester to Trent, are behind the fencing to the left.

Midland Counties Railway

Fundamentally, the idea for a line arose from the desire of coal owners in the Erewash Valley for cheap transportation of their product to the market in Leicester. The opening of the Leicester & Swannington Railway in 1832 had brought cheap coal into the town. However, during the ensuing preliminaries, opposition from the embryo North Midland Company and from local canal owners caused the proposition for a line along the Erewash Valley to be abandoned, so the Act which received Royal Assent on 21st June 1836 authorised a railway from Nottingham to Derby and to Rugby from a junction at Long Eaton.

Initial efforts were concentrated on constructing the line from Derby to Nottingham, which opened to public services on 4th June 1839 from a temporary platform at Derby, the North Midland station not having been completed.

The Trent (Long Eaton) to Rugby line opened in two stages in 1840, the Northern part to Leicester on 4th May, preceding the Leicester to Rugby portion by two months.

Plate 192: The bridge number is painted on the brick pier of the footbridge on the left in this view of Kegworth.

Plate 193: Hathern. The goods lines are to the left of this view looking south. The structures are by now a familiar sight, the main building being similar to King's Norton, Duffield, etc. The waiting shelter is the cross gable type, and the footbridge is as detailed at Yate *(Figure 1)*.

B. Hilton

Plates 194 & 195: Loughborough. In the view (seen below), looking towards Leicester (*Plate 195*), the awning is shown to advantage, and the ironwork for this, with lattice cross members supported by filigree brackets from slender fluted columns, was produced by Richards of Leicester. Comparison should be made with *Figure 15 & Plate 154* in *A Pictorial Record of LMS Architecture* (Melton Mowbray). This type was arguably one of the most attractive produced for the Midland Railway, and contrasted strongly with the solid though pleasing proportions of the structure facing the town, although an additional display of glass and iron covered the passenger entrance (*Plate 194*).

L&GRP, Courtesy David & Charles

Plate 195

Plate 196: Barrow-on-Soar & Quorn was opened as Barrow by the Midland Counties Railway, whose original building with similarities to that detailed in *Figure 19*, is to the right. This early view was photographed looking south, after the provision of goods lines, but before replacement of the Midland 'short window' signal box.

Plate 197: A view of Sileby, looking south, in April 1914. If one could describe the 'typical' Midland wooden station building, Sileby would undoubtedly be a prominent example. However, although the design was not widespread, features such as extended eaves, central screen waiting area, and diagonal and vertical panelling were well-known. One suspects that the Midland Counties stone-edged platform has been elevated by the use of brick, to form a coping. The use of brick was not as usually found. The rudimentary waiting shelter on the 'up' platform resembles the one in a similar position at Barrow-on-Soar (*Plate 196*) and at Scotby (*Plate 126*).

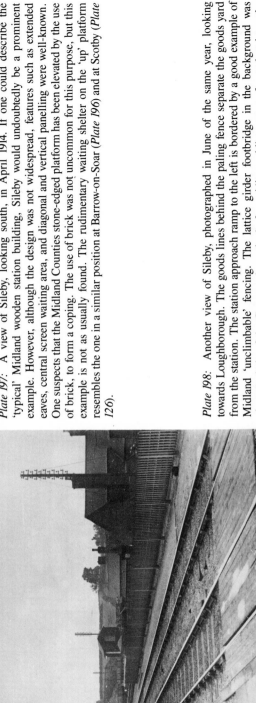

Plate 198: Another view of Sileby, photographed in June of the same year, looking towards Loughborough. The goods lines behind the paling fence separate the goods yard from the station. The station approach ramp to the left is bordered by a good example of Midland 'unclimbable' fencing. The lattice girder footbridge in the background was characteristic of the Company's method of providing public passage for pedestrians, the overhead wind bracing being the most ... iar feature.

Leicester

Plate 199: Some eight years before work was necessary at Nottingham, the growth of the city of Leicester had prompted the Midland Railway to renew their station. The handsome classical building fronting Campbell Street, a little north of the present site, which the Midland Counties Railway had provided, started with one platform handling 'up' and 'down' trains. By 1859, a further platform had been added. On 12th June 1892, this was superseded by the London Road Station. Mr MacDonald was the Engineer for the Company and the design was by Mr C. Trubshaw, the Company Architect. Two 'up' and two 'down' platforms were provided on two islands, between which was a single span glazed roof. The two outer platforms had the benefit of ridge and furrow canopies, cantilevered from the building on heavy built-up beams (*see A Pictorial Record of LMS Architecture — Plate 161*). The main entrance at street level was into an imposing edifice in brick and orange brown terracotta capped by balustrading, the parapet of which was surmounted by a series of urns. The scene was highlighted by an imposing hexagonal clock tower.

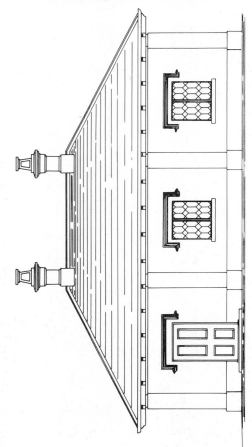

ELEVATION NEXT PLATFORM

M.C.R.
WIGSTON STATION

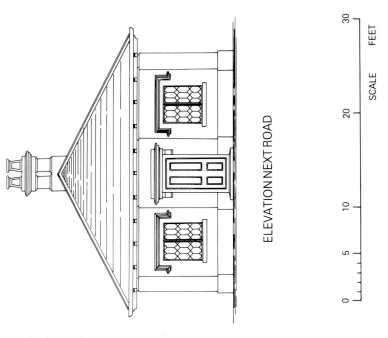

ELEVATION NEXT ROAD

0 5 10 20 30

SCALE FEET

Plate 200: Countesthorpe, on the line from Leicester to Rugby, shows clearly the type of alterations carried out. Only the left wing of the original building exists, whilst at Wigston, it was the right wing. Note once again the 'standard' Midland level crossing gates.

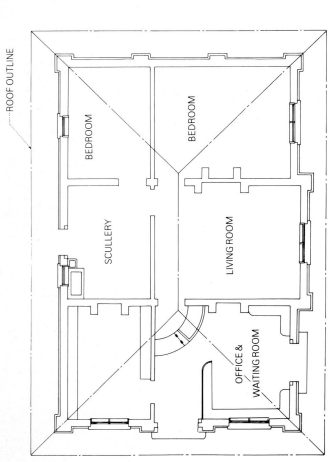

ROOF OUTLINE

BEDROOM

BEDROOM

SCULLERY

LIVING ROOM

OFFICE & WAITING ROOM

PLAN

Figure 19: This diagram is based on an original Midland Counties Railway drawing intended for Wigston Station on the Leicester to Rugby section of the line which opened in 1840. The building, in this form, was actually constructed, but later altered almost beyond recognition. Probably the best example of a building with these design features was Barrow (later Barrow-on-Soar & Quorn) (*Plate 196*) which survived, albeit externally

Leicester to Hitchin

In looking for alternative routes to London, independent of the LNWR who had occasional delays at Rugby, the Midland Railway took up a scheme first introduced by an independent company whose proposals had been rejected by Parliament in 1846.

The following year, the Midland Railway resubmitted the plans for a line to run from Leicester to the Great Northern Railway at Hitchin, taking in Wellingborough and Bedford, and received the necessary powers. Financial stringency caused delays, but authorisation was reviewed on 4th August 1853. The building of the line was entrusted to the contractor Thomas Brassey, although John Knowles was responsible for the only original tunnel, at Warden. Coincidentally in 1846, the Eastern Counties Railway, an ally of the Midland Railway, had submitted plans for an extension to Hitchin. Although authorisation was refused, the Midland Railway were actively prevented by Parliament from crossing the Great Northern Railway to join such a line. The Leicester to Hitchin line was opened throughout in 1857, in April for coal traffic, on 4th May for goods, with passenger traffic commencing four days later.

Much of the traffic from the larger towns had already been tapped by the LNWR and its predecessors, with cross-country branches through Wellingborough to Peterborough, Bletchley to Bedford, and Rugby to Market Harborough. However, the new Midland line was able to offer a shorter route to the capital. As can be seen from the examples shown, the original stations, designed by G. H. Driver, had a similar theme, with the stationmaster's house being flanked by a single storey office extension. The platform side formed a brick enclosed waiting shelter with a ridge and furrow roof. At the larger stations of Wellingborough and Kettering, this ridge and furrow extended over the platform as a glass awning. This type of glass and iron awning made its first appearance on the Midland Railway at these locations, their inspiration being from Sir Joseph Paxton, a Midland Railway Director, and from the Crystal Palace.

At Bedford Station, accommodation was shared with the LNWR for a time until it could be agreed which site should be used for the Midland's new station. This finally opened on 1st February 1859, using similar designs already employed on the line. The Midland Railway's feeling for local materials is clearly shown along the length of the Leicester to Hitchin line, varying from yellow brick to the south, red brick at Bedford and Kibworth, white brick at Great Glen, and limestone at Glendon and Rushton.

Plate 201: The building at Wigston (named Magna by the LMS) seems to be a late addition, and was resplendent with ball finials and mouldings, and proudly carried the name 'MR Wigston Station' carved above an entrance with ornate iron gates. The attractive stonework to the front was omitted on the side gables, which exhibit a more austere aspect. Unfortunately, the far chimney stack has been reconstructed.
L&GRP, Courtesy David & Charles

Plate 202: Great Glen. This was an original Leicester & Hitchin Railway building constructed in local white brick, the large house being flanked by an office extension in a basic 'T' shape. Once again, the large size of the nameboard is evident, by reference to the members of staff standing adjacent to it. As the prefix 'Great' was not added until 1897, perhaps the sign is contemporary with the photograph. The staff have obviously spent a great deal of time preparing a splendid garden.

Plate 203: A view of East Langton, looking north. The heavily-valanced wooden building and sloping-roofed waiting shelter are of types seen before in our travels around the Midland system (e.g. Berkeley Road). Note the goods van body, used to extend accommodation. Compare the more usual method of completing brick platforms with that mentioned at Sileby (*Plate 197*).
L&GRP, Courtesy David & Charles

Plate 204 (above): A summer scene at Glendon & Rushton, photographed in August 1915, prior to the reconstruction of the bridge in the foreground; work that was obviously necessary to upgrade the capacity of the line, perhaps as a wartime measure. The three wrought-iron main girders and cross girders supporting longitudinal timbers were to be replaced by a fabricated steel bridge of unit construction. The deck of the new bridge would allow ordinary ballasted track to be laid.

Plate 205 (opposite): In this view, photographed in November 1915, the new bridge has been erected on trestles in readiness for rolling in after the removal of the old structure. The outside girders formed a walkway on which railings were attached. (These views should be compared with those in *A Pictorial Record of LMS Architecture* — *Plate 458*). Mentioned should be made of the Leicester & Hitchin Railway buildings, here built in limestone. Note the ridge and furrow waiting shelter on the 'up' platform, a style repeated at other locations, echoing the roof line of the waiting area of the office extension to the main building.

M.R. Kettering.

—Station Buildings.—

Extensive reconstruction at the beginning of the 1890s witnessed the removal of the original Leicester & Hitchin station buildings. These were replaced by the now familiar brick and terracotta features. Mr G. Biddle attributed the design to Charles Trubshaw.

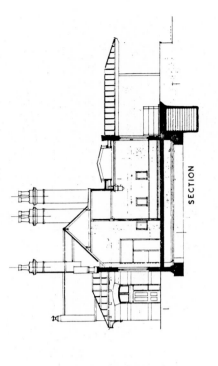

SECTION

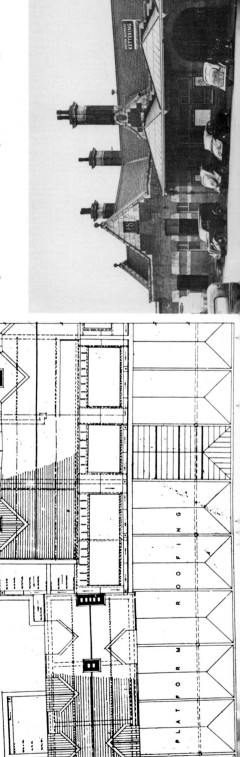

Figure 20: Elevations and a plan of the buildings as reconstructed in 1890.

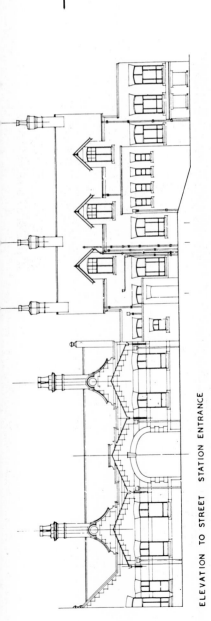

ELEVATION TO STREET   STATION ENTRANCE

ELEVATION TO PLATFORM

PLATFORM   ROOFING

Kettering

Plate 207 (right): Kettering, showing an early view after reconstruction of the Leicester end of the island platform canopy.

Plate 206 (opposite): This illustrates the Station Street entrance of Kettering Station with its canopy cantilevered from the building on rolled section joists. A similar shallow-pitched canopy on the platform was supported by cast columns, similar to those shown in *Figure 16*. The island platform came into being on completion of the quadrupling in 1884. Simple facilities were provided by wooden prefabricated buildings (*Figure 21*) below a large area of glass and iron. The original canopy was extended by the addition of 'facsimile' ironwork which should be compared with *Figure 22*, at Wellingborough. The outer platform on the 'down' fast line was similarly treated.

BR/OPC Joint Venture

Plate 208 (lower right): Kettering. The iron tracery is shown to good advantage in this view. The main building to the right dates from the 1890s, with canopies of the ridge and furrow type with hipped ends, in contrast to the gabled ends of the island and outer platform canopies.

L&GRP, Courtesy David & Charles

Figure 21: An elevation and plan of the island platform building and canopy, from an original drawing.

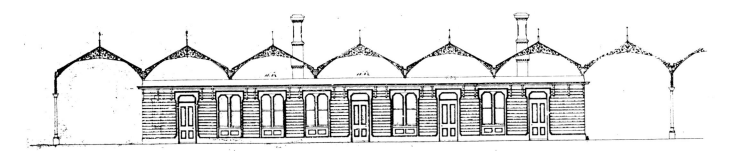

Elevation of Station Buildings. B.

Plan.

Wellingborough

Plate 209: Wellingborough, showing a view looking north from the 'up' fast platform. The later slow lines are to the right, the footbridge over which was extended in 1894.

Until quadrupling of the line, Wellingborough retained its Leicester & Hitchin building, virtually untouched. Enlargement of the station resulted in the provision of the island platform and slow lines on the 'down' side. Contemporary with the enclosing of the footbridge was the extension, in 1883, of the canopies at the south end of the main building. This was executed again with ironwork to the same pattern as the original, as in *Figure 22*.

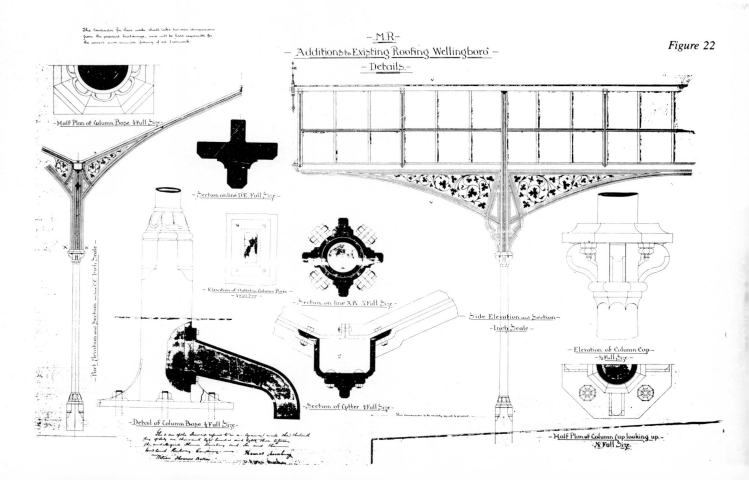

Figure 22

Plates 210 & 211: Irchester. The main station building at Irchester was located on a part of the overbridge spanning the passenger lines. The half-timbered mock Tudor with herring-bone brickwork seemed to be popular with the Midland Railway at this time, similar examples having been seen at Burton upon Trent and Calverley. The waiting shelter is virtually a repeat of those at Sileby and Battow-on-Soar, but with diagonal infill panels.

Plate 210 BR/OPC Joint Venture

Plate 212: Oakley. This view well illustrates the Leicester & Hitchin building detail and, in particular, the ridge and furrow roof covering the waiting area, and the typical round-topped windows in pairs can be seen. It is notable that the waiting shelter on the 'up' platform and the coal merchant's offices at the goods yard entrance are executed in the same vein. At this location, red brick was used for the construction.

P. Herniman

The London Extension

For some years the Leicester & Hitchin Railway allowed the Midland Railway easy access to London by using GNR metals south of Hitchin, but inevitably as business increased on the Great Northern and Midland routes, delays were occasioned, and preference was naturally given to GNR trains. This, together with the enormous sum of £¼ million paid in tolls to the GNR and LNWR for passage over their lines, prompted the Midland Railway's Board to approach Parliament about a London extension. The Act of 22nd June 1863 gave powers for a line to commence at a junction with the L&H at the north end of Bedford Station, and to run via Luton and St. Albans to St. Pancras. In addition, there was to be a branch from Kentish Town to King's Cross on the Metropolitan Railway.

Two tracks were initially laid, except for the last few miles into London where four were provided, but provision was made during construction for two additional lines. Even the bridges were built for four tracks.

Goods traffic commenced in September 1867 to the existing St. Pancras goods station which had opened in 1865 on a spur from King's Cross (GNR). Passenger trains from Bedford started to use the underground lines to Moorgate on the Metropolitan Railway's widened lines in July 1868. St. Pancras passenger station opened for business in October of the same year. Four tracks were available throughout, with the opening of the second tunnels at Elstree and Ampthill in 1895. A second Belsize Tunnel had opened in 1884.

Stations on the London extension were of two basic types. For the northern contract, a style similar to that of the Leicester & Hitchin Railway was employed, with either a house or large office block forming the head of the 'T'.

At Ampthill, the stationmaster's house was separated from the station. Being quite an important centre, a larger station received the 1868 version of the hipped end ridge and furrow awning carried on extensive intricate cast brackets (*see Plate 216*).

At the road side entrance (*Plate 215*) the roof line was extended to form a canopy edge by saw-toothed valancing. Note the variety of window headings, all executed in stone.

Plate 213: A view of Bedford, looking north, towards the junction of the London extension. The station opened at Bedford in 1859, using buildings of a similar design to other Leicester & Hitchin stations, utilising iron and glass canopies of the same type as those fitted at Kettering and Wellingborough. With the opening of the London extension in 1868, the main line through Bedford was aligned a little to the west. The building of the new platform and offices was carried out to harmonise with the old structure. The glazed awning utilised the same materials and design in spite of the use of modernised techniques at other locations. The through lines of the Hitchin route were cut to provide a passenger concourse, creating north and south facing bays.

Plate 214: This view shows the southern (Hitchin) bay in 1968, and well illustrates the additional roofing provided over the passenger area. To the left can be seen the saw-toothed top to the outer wall of the original station.

H. C. Casserley Collection

ate 215: Ampthill.   *H. C. Casserley*

te 216: Ampthill.   *BR/OPC Joint Venture*

e 217 : Flitwick, although similar in
cept, did not in fact open until 1870. Here, the
onmaster's house was part of the station build-
. The utility building, to the left, resembles
y of the timber structures seen on our travels.

e 218: Leagrave was one of the original
ons with an integral house. The waiting shel-
on the 'up' platform to the left is of a type
e found widely on this line. In later years,
goods lines behind the 'up' platform were to
ive platform faces and, at the same time, the
oridge was relocated and extended.

Luton

Plate 219: Luton. A public thoroughfare crossed the Midland and the Great Northern railways on a footbridge. The Midland Railway effectively utilised this as a subsidiary station entrance, as well as for platform interchange.

Plate 220: Luton. The portion of the footbridge crossing over the station approach road. The Midland station is to the left and the Great Northern station to the right.

Plate 221: Luton. Very extensive ridge and furrow awnings were provided for the benefit of the Luton public, and much of the canopy over the island platform is devoid of building but indicates that protection was required for large numbers of passengers. The train on the right is for Moorgate and will pass through the tunnel under St. Pancras Station on to the Metropolitan Railway's widened lines. In the 1930s, this station was completely rebuilt by the LMS (*see A Pictorial Record of LMS Architecture — Plates 318-321*). A fourth platform was added to the slow lines in BR days.

Harpenden

Plate 222

Plate 223

Plate 224

Plate 225

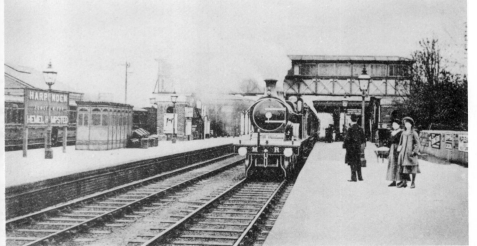

Plate 226

Plate 222: The road approach to Harpenden Station at the turn of the century. Behind the photographer is an entrance block almost identical to that at Ampthill (*see Plate 215*).
BR/OPC Joint Venture

Plate 223: The 'down' fast platform at Harpenden, with the same format as at Ampthill, although at some time repairs to the awning have resulted in hipped ends being provided. Note the ornate stone window heading and patterned barge board to the gabled office.
BR/OPC Joint Venture

Plate 224: The 'up' slow platform was a later addition, and received timber buildings similar to the ones detailed at West Hampstead (*Figures 24 & 25*) although in this case, plate steel brackets replaced steel angular struts as roof supports.
BR/OPC Joint Venture

Plate 225: The building on the island platform is of the style seen at Leagrave, but with a flat roof, as it stands beneath an umbrella canopy. The roof brackets are again as at Ampthill and on the 'down' platform here at Harpenden.
BR/OPC Joint Venture

Plate 226: An interesting view of Harpenden before the footbridge was extended for the installation of the 'up' slow platform.

Plate 228

Plate 227: This view of Radlett is included to illustrate the construction detail of the large angled nameboards which we have seen at so many locations.

Plate 228: Radlett Station was virtually a copy of Harpenden in every detail.

Plate 229: Elstree was the first station on the southern contract for the London extension, and received a different kind of building, a type fully described in *A Pictorial Record of LMS Architecture — Plates 121-124*. A different ridge and furrow appeared with gabled ends but of shallower pitch than at Kettering etc., and a different type of bracket.

Plates 230 & 231: Hendon. Platform detail was similar to other locations and indeed like Elstree, but the elevated position of the road-level entrance demanded a different layout to accommodate the necessary access to the footbridge which linked the platforms.

Plate 230 H. C. Casserley Collection

Plate 229

Plate 231

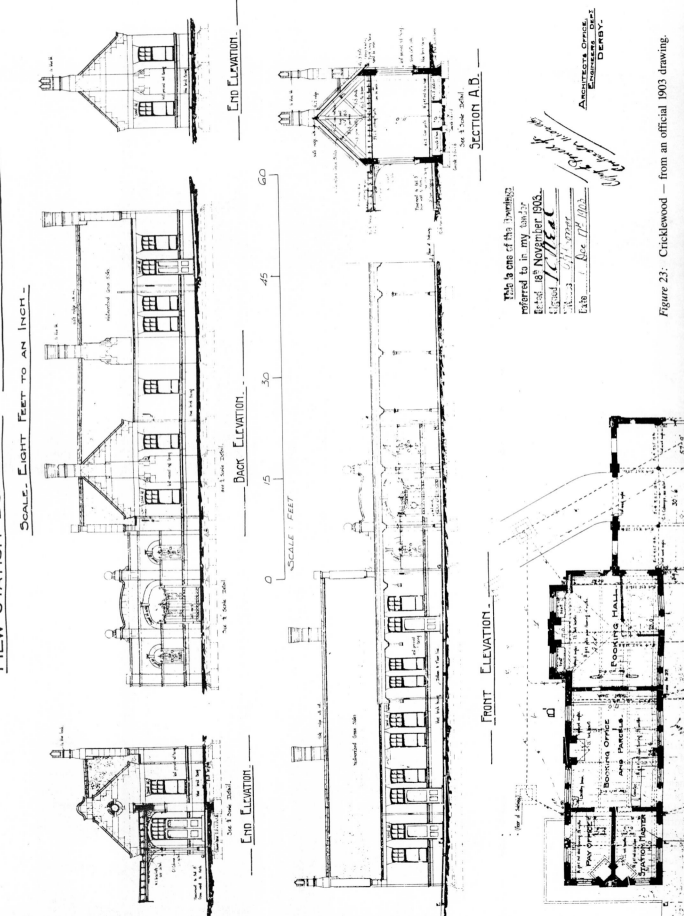

Figure 23: Cricklewood — from an official 1903 drawing.

Cricklewood

Plate 232: Looking south, the goods lines are to the extreme right. On the left are the sidings serving the Express Dairies.

Plate 233: The buildings at platform level are a mixture of brick and timber, with large flat canopies having certain similarities to the structures found on the slow platforms on the southern section of the London extension. Compare this view with Harpenden (*Plate 224*). The station was first opened in 1870 as Child's Hill.

Cricklewood Station tended to be overshadowed by the facilities of its better-known counterparts, the locomotive and rolling stock sheds and goods sorting sidings. However, one of the Company's small attractive stations was produced as a result of alterations detailed in the 1903 drawing (*Figure 23*). Although not possessing too much embellishment, attention to detail was focused on the entrance building which was constructed in dark reddish brown terracotta, with moulded brickwork. The gable ends received ball finials in a manner similar to others illustrated previously, namely Rotherham (*Plate 165*), Wigston Magna (*Plate 201*), and Kettering (*Plate 206*).

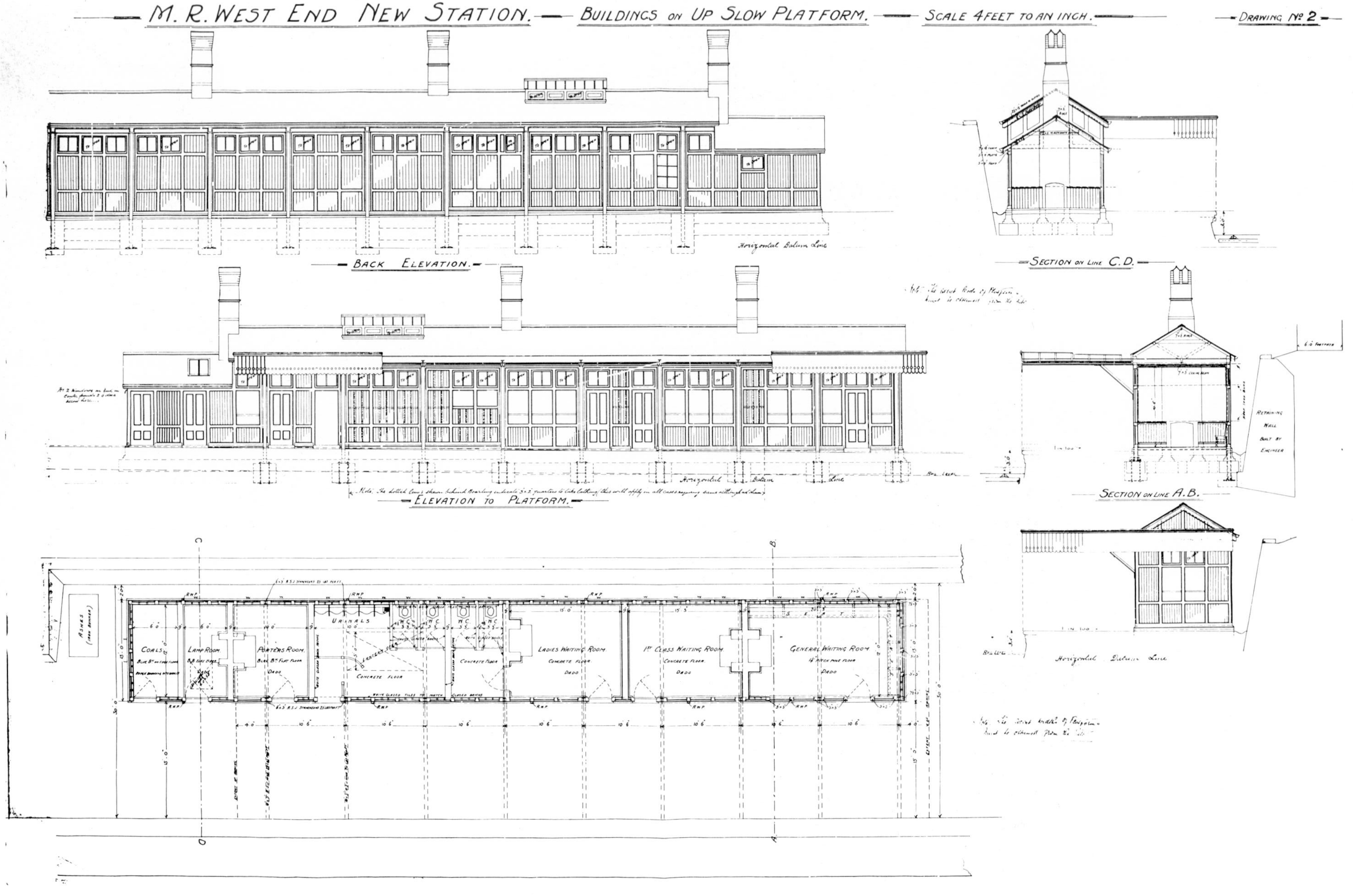

Figure 24: Elevations and plan for the new station at West End.

M.R. West End New Station.

Buildings on Down Slow and Island Platforms.

Scale 4 feet to one inch.

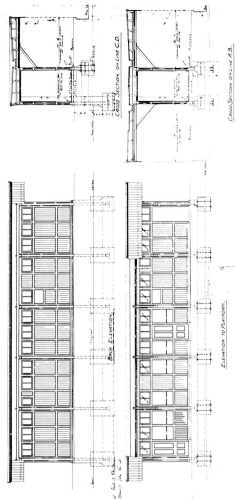

Cross Section on line C.D.

Cross Section on line A.B.

Back Elevation.

Elevation to Platform.

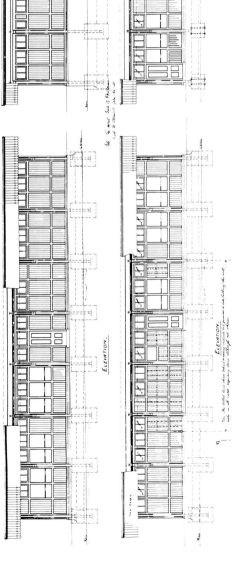

Elevation.

Elevation.

Figure 25: Elevations from an original drawing, showing details of the island platform buildings.

Plate 234: A station had existed at this location since 1871, but with the quadrupling was greatly enlarged to the form detailed in this view looking north. The steel-framed/timber-panelled buildings were of a design repeated at numerous locations. The outer platform to the right serves the 'up' slow line, whilst the fast lines are to the left of the island platform. The station, by this time, had been renamed West Hampstead (from September 1905). The island platform buildings were of a much lighter appearance than their outer platform counterparts, the Westmorland slated roofing giving way to lightweight zinc-plated canopies.

Plate 235: At road level, the Company provided a series of attractive shop fronts, pictured in this view, again finished with reddish brown terracotta and MR initials. This 1906 view shows the station entrance to the right.

Plate 236: Finchley Road. The entrance at road level to the relatively short-lived Finchley Road Station. This, the second station to bear this name, was opened in February 1884 and closed on 11th July 1927. The Midland Railway constructed a pleasing crescent-shaped entrance in light stone, with small offices and shops around the perimeter. Of the numerous coal merchants renting these premises, one can be forgiven for thinking that the Stanley Wallsend Coal Co. was the most publicity conscious, having displayed its name in no less than six places.

St. Pancras

In the environs of St. Pancras, the Midland Railway provided extensive facilities for the delivery of coal to the capital. Shortly before entering the terminus, one passes the Cambridge Street and Regent Canal coal depots.

Plate 237 (above): Cambridge Street. This shows the Midland coal bays in the foreground and the GNR opposite. The latter were in the process of reconstructing the bays and awnings.

BR/OPC Joint Venture

Plate 238 (below): Regent Canal. A barge is being loaded at the Cambridge Street Hanging Depot. It is interesting to note that with the line of wagons above the discharge hoppers is a Signal Department vehicle.

BR/OPC Joint Venture

Plate 239: A drivers view of the approach to St. Pancras Station. Within a month of this May 1914 view, the 42 signals had been reduced to 16 by substituting Messrs Acfield and Cooke's route indicators. The handsome profile of the train shed dominates the background. Note the dual-standard loading gauge hanging from the gantry.

ST PANCRAS MAY 1914

St. Pancras

The St. Pancras terminus of the London extension came into use on 1st October 1868. Six thousand men, one thousand horses and one hundred steam cranes worked for four years to erect the station and hotel, completely dwarfing the station of the two Midland Railway rivals to east and west at King's Cross and Euston.

Clearing the site for the railway caused the removal of the desolate and miserable slum at Agar Town.

The station itself, noted for its roof which, in a single arched span, 240ft. wide x 100ft. high x 690ft. long, covering four acres, was the responsibility of the Midland Railway Engineer Mr W. K. Barlow. The interior was free from internal walls and supports, allowing maximum use to be made of the space.

A colossal wooden scaffolding, running on rails, was utilised during the construction of the roof. This could be moved by an army of workmen using crowbars, working in unison to the beat of a gong. The timber of this scaffolding was later cut into blocks and utilised in the carriageway from Euston Road.

Forming the imposing Gothic facade to the station was the handsome St. Pancras Hotel (later to be called the Midland Grand Hotel) which opened in May 1873, built to the designs of Sir George Gilbert Scott, the eminent architect, and displaying a wealth of pinnacled towers, pointed arches, iron balconies, and rows of pointed dormers. Once the last word in luxury, glory departed from the 400 bedroom hotel in 1935 when the LMS converted the building into offices.

On the St. Pancras approach, the railway had to be raised to cross the Regent Canal, and because of this Barlow elected to build an elevated terminus, and made use of the ground beneath to create a vast goods warehouse. This was used principally for the handling of beer from Burton on Trent, traffic fostered as early as 1843 by the Birmingham & Derby Junction Railway. The roof of this cellar, built of wrought-iron cross girders, formed the ties between the feet of the main ribs springing from brick piers at floor level of the passenger station. Wagons were carried to the cellar by hydraulic lift.

Plate 240

Plate 241

Plate 242

Plate 243

Plate 240: The train shed in the process of being constructed.

Plate 241: Finishing touches are being applied, but the hotel is yet incomplete. Also still missing is the station clock.

Plate 242: A view through the train shed from the hotel end. The later platforms, 3 and 4, were yet to be provided.

Plate 243: A view looking along platform 2 from the booking hall end, at the height of the Midland period.

INDEX

Plate 245: The entrance to St. Pancras Station on Euston Road, in April 1904. By 1908 the massive gates had been removed, leaving only the ornate posts with the legends IN and OUT on them. The pitched roof shelter was also removed, being replaced by a smaller version (*see A Pictorial Record of LMS Architecure — Plate 112*). The exit gates are to the extreme left.